BeagleBone By Example

Learn how to build physical computing systems using
BeagleBone Black and Python

Jayakarthigeyan Prabakar

PUBLISHING

BIRMINGHAM - MUMBAI

BeagleBone By Example

First published: August 2016

Production reference: 1290816

Published by Packt Publishing Ltd.
Livery Place
35 Livery Street
Birmingham B3 2PB, UK.

ISBN 978-1-78528-505-9

www.packtpub.com

Image source:- BeagleBoard.org Foundation (http://beagleboard.org/)

Credits

Author
Jayakarthigeyan Prabakar

Reviewer
Christopher Rush

Acquisition Editor
Rahul Nair

Content Development Editor
Trusha Shriyan

Technical Editor
Nirant Carvalho

Copy Editor
Sneha Singh
Safis Editing

Project Coordinator
Shweta H Birwatkar

Proofreader
Safis Editing

Indexer
Hemangini Bari

Graphics
Kirk D'Penha

Production Coordinator
Shantanu N. Zagade

Cover Work
Shantanu N. Zagade

About the Author

Jayakarthigeyan Prabakar is an electrical and electronics engineer with more than three years of experience in real-time embedded systems development. He loves building cloud-connected physical computing systems using Arduino, MSP430, Raspberry Pi, BeagleBone Black, Intel Edison, ESP8266 and more.

Jayakarthigeyan started understanding how computing devices and operating systems work when he started repairing his personal computer on his own in middle school that is when he first got his hands on in electronics.

From his third year in the undergraduate degree program, he started building prototypes for various start-ups around the world as a freelancer. Currently, Jayakarthigeyan is a full-time technical lead of the R & D division in a Home Automation startup and works as a consultant to many other companies involved in Robotics, Industrial Automation and other IoT solutions as well; he helps build prototypes to bring their ideas to reality.

I would like to dedicate this book to those two strong and wonderful women in my life, my mother Saraswathi and my wife Shivaranjani for believing in me and always encouraging me to do what I like with my crazy ideas.

Thanks to my grandfather Alavandar who has influenced and shaped me to what I am today. Special thanks to Rahul Nair for giving me the opportunity to write this book. Thanks to Mamata Walkar, Trusha Shriyan, Nirant Carvalho and all others at Packt Publishing for their support to me in shaping this book.

About the Reviewer

Christopher Rush is from Preston, UK. He has a degree in computer science and has spent the last 15 years working in the electronics industry. Christopher is a full-time technical consultant and has an extensive knowledge of the maker industry. Chris is a regular blogger on MAKER.IO (`https://www.maker.io/`) providing tutorials and guides for popular development boards such as Arduino, Raspberry Pi, BeagleBone, and many more. Chris is also the Author of 30 *BeagleBone Black Projects for the Evil Geniu*, *Programming the Particle Photon: Getting started with the Internet of Things*, and *Programming the Intel Galileo: Getting started with Internet-Connected Hardware*.

www.PacktPub.com

eBooks, discount offers, and more

Did you know that Packt offers eBook versions of every book published, with PDF and ePub files available? You can upgrade to the eBook version at www.PacktPub.com and as a print book customer, you are entitled to a discount on the eBook copy. Get in touch with us at customercare@packtpub.com for more details.

At www.PacktPub.com, you can also read a collection of free technical articles, sign up for a range of free newsletters and receive exclusive discounts and offers on Packt books and eBooks.

https://www2.packtpub.com/books/subscription/packtlib

Do you need instant solutions to your IT questions? PacktLib is Packt's online digital book library. Here, you can search, access, and read Packt's entire library of books.

Why subscribe?

- Fully searchable across every book published by Packt
- Copy and paste, print, and bookmark content
- On demand and accessible via a web browser

Table of Contents

Preface

If you are among those who are looking for a simple step-by-step guide to learn basic electronics and start interfacing sensors and actuators with a low-cost Linux development board, such as BeagleBone Black through examples to build internet connected physical computing systems and robots. This book is for you to get started if you have prior knowledge of basic python programming and little understanding of how a computer works.

What this book covers

Chapter 1, *Get Started with BeagleBone* , tells us about the hardware specification of the BeagleBone board, how to set up a BeagleBone board to boot up with a Linux Operating System on microSD card and log in to the Linux command shell from a remote computer, and how to program on Python software running on the BeagleBone board.

Chapter 2, *Circuit Fundaments and GPIO*, talks about the working of basic electronic circuits including switches, LEDs, and battery followed by GPIO pins on the BeagleBone board and elaborates on how you can use these GPIO pins to switch LED status using a python program.

Chapter 3, *Introduction to Physical Computing Systems*, helps you understand the basic structure of physical computing systems with real world examples, build your own physical computing system using a switch as an input and LED as the output device connected to BeagleBone board which works based on the python program that you write.

Chapter 4, *Real-Time physical computing systems Using BeagleBone Board*, talks about analog sensors using LM35 temperature sensor as an example and works on a more advanced physical computing project using BeagleBone board interfaced with an LM35.

Chapter 5, Connecting Physical Computing Systems to the Internet, teaches you how to connect BeagleBone board to Wi-Fi networks, cloud storage and upload sensor data from BeagleBone board to cloud in real-time, and view the trends on the cloud software with time stamps. Build your first IoT.

Chapter 6, Home Automation Using BeagleBone, tells you about how to set up your own web server on a BeagleBone board using a Python and Flask framework and how to use the same to control home appliances using an AC relay board interfaced with BeagleBone board from a PC or your mobile phone connected to the internet, similar to any other IoT Home Automation system.

Chapter 7, Working with Images Using Computer Vision, teaches you how to interface a USB camera with BeagleBone board and how to OpenCV to capture images and work with them using Python.

Chapter 8, Home Security Systems Using BeagleBone Black, teaches us how to use SMTP with python to send emails, learn about PIR sensors and motion detection, build a smart intruder alert system by interfacing PIR sensor with BeagleBone board to detect motion, and use OpenCV to capture images and email them.

Chapter 9, Exploring Robotics, helps you understand the basic structure of robotic systems, their working and application in different areas using real life examples. It also helps us learn about differential drive robots

Chapter 10, Building Your Own Robot, teaches us about DC Motors, Motor Driver IC L293D and control of DC motors from Python on BeagleBone Black using this Motor Driver IC, live streaming of video on local server from USB camera connected to BeagleBone board, and building your own Tele Controlled Robot with live video streaming.

What you need for this book

Basic Python programming knowledge and little understanding of how a computer works in terms of the electronics inside it.

Who this book is for

This book is for those who are looking for a simple step by step guide to learn basic electronics and start interfacing sensors and actuators, with a low-cost Linux development board like BeagleBone Black through examples to build IoT and Robot Systems

Conventions

In this book, you will find a number of text styles that distinguish between different kinds of information. Here are some examples of these styles and an explanation of their meaning.

Code words in text, database table names, folder names, filenames, file extensions, pathnames, dummy URLs, user input, and Twitter handles are shown as follows: "Let's power off our BeagleBone board using the command `sudo poweroff`, which will shut down the operating system."

A block of code is set as follows:

```
<img src="http://192.168.2.42:8080/?action=stream">
```

Any command-line input or output is written as follows:

```
sudo python Blink.py
```

New terms and **important words** are shown in bold. Words that you see on the screen, for example, in menus or dialog boxes, appear in the text like this: "Click on **Yes** and continue."

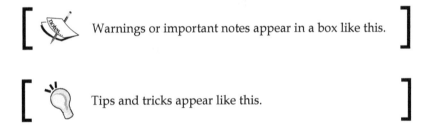

> Warnings or important notes appear in a box like this.

> Tips and tricks appear like this.

Reader feedback

Feedback from our readers is always welcome. Let us know what you think about this book—what you liked or disliked. Reader feedback is important for us as it helps us develop titles that you will really get the most out of.

To send us general feedback, simply e-mail feedback@packtpub.com, and mention the book's title in the subject of your message.

If there is a topic that you have expertise in and you are interested in either writing or contributing to a book, see our author guide at www.packtpub.com/authors.

Customer support

Now that you are the proud owner of a Packt book, we have a number of things to help you to get the most from your purchase.

Downloading the example code

You can download the example code files for this book from your account at `http://www.packtpub.com`. If you purchased this book elsewhere, you can visit `http://www.packtpub.com/support` and register to have the files e-mailed directly to you.

You can download the code files by following these steps:

1. Log in or register to our website using your e-mail address and password.
2. Hover the mouse pointer on the **SUPPORT** tab at the top.
3. Click on **Code Downloads & Errata**.
4. Enter the name of the book in the **Search** box.
5. Select the book for which you're looking to download the code files.
6. Choose from the drop-down menu where you purchased this book from.
7. Click on **Code Download**.

You can also download the code files by clicking on the **Code Files** button on the book's webpage at the Packt Publishing website. This page can be accessed by entering the book's name in the **Search** box. Please note that you need to be logged in to your Packt account.

Once the file is downloaded, please make sure that you unzip or extract the folder using the latest version of:

- WinRAR / 7-Zip for Windows
- Zipeg / iZip / UnRarX for Mac
- 7-Zip / PeaZip for Linux

The code bundle for the book is also hosted on GitHub at `https://github.com/PacktPublishing/BeagleBone-By-Example`. We also have other code bundles from our rich catalog of books and videos available at `https://github.com/PacktPublishing/`. Check them out!

Errata

Although we have taken every care to ensure the accuracy of our content, mistakes do happen. If you find a mistake in one of our books—maybe a mistake in the text or the code—we would be grateful if you could report this to us. By doing so, you can save other readers from frustration and help us improve subsequent versions of this book. If you find any errata, please report them by visiting http://www.packtpub.com/submit-errata, selecting your book, clicking on the **Errata Submission Form** link, and entering the details of your errata. Once your errata are verified, your submission will be accepted and the errata will be uploaded to our website or added to any list of existing errata under the Errata section of that title.

To view the previously submitted errata, go to https://www.packtpub.com/books/content/support and enter the name of the book in the search field. The required information will appear under the **Errata** section.

Piracy

Piracy of copyrighted material on the Internet is an ongoing problem across all media. At Packt, we take the protection of our copyright and licenses very seriously. If you come across any illegal copies of our works in any form on the Internet, please provide us with the location address or website name immediately so that we can pursue a remedy.

Please contact us at copyright@packtpub.com with a link to the suspected pirated material.

We appreciate your help in protecting our authors and our ability to bring you valuable content.

Questions

If you have a problem with any aspect of this book, you can contact us at questions@packtpub.com, and we will do our best to address the problem.

1
Getting Started with BeagleBone

If you are reading this book right now, it means that you have taken your first step to get started with your BeagleBone board to build real-time physical computing systems using your BeagleBone board and Python programming language. This chapter will teach you how to set up your BeagleBone board for the first time and write your first few Python codes on it.

By end of this book, you would have learned the basics of interfacing electronics to BeagleBone boards and coding it using Python which will allow you to build almost anything from a home automation system to a robot through examples given in this book.

Firstly, in this chapter, you will learn how to set up your BeagleBone board for the first time with a new operating system, followed by usage of some basic Linux Shell commands that will help you out while we work on the Shell Terminal to write and execute python codes and do much more like installing different libraries and software on your BeagleBone board. Once you get familiar with usage of the Linux terminal, you will write your first code on python that will run on your BeagleBone board. Once you are comfortable with that, we will modify the code to make it do something more in the next chapters. Most of the time, we will be using the freely available open-source codes and libraries available on the Internet to write programs on top of it and using it to make the program work for our requirement instead of entirely writing a code from scratch to build our embedded systems using BeagleBone board. The contents of this chapter are divided into the following sections:

- Prerequisites
- About the single board computer - BeagleBone board
- Know your BeagleBone board

- Setting up your BeagleBone board
- Working on Linux Shell
- Coding on Python in BeagleBone board

Prerequisites

This topic will cover what parts you need to get started with BeagleBone Black. You can buy them online or pick them up from any electronics store that is available in your locality.

The following is the list of materials needed to get started:

- 1x BeagleBone Black
- 1x miniUSB type B to type A cable
- 1x microSD Card (4 GB or More)
- 1x microSD Card Reader
- 1x 5V DC, 2A Power Supply
- 1x Ethernet Cable

There are different variants of BeagleBone boards like BeagleBone, BeagleBone Black, BeagleBone Green and some more old variants. This book will mostly have the BeagleBone Black shown in the pictures. Note that BeagleBone Black can replace any of the other BeagleBone boards such as the BeagleBone or BeagleBone Green for most of the projects. These boards have their own extra features so to say. For example, the BeagleBone Black has more RAM, it has almost double the size of RAM available in BeagleBone and an in-built eMMC to store operating system instead of booting it up only through operating system installed on microSD card in BeagleBone White. Keeping in mind that this book should be able to guide people with most of the BeagleBone board variants, the tutorials in this book will be based on operating system booted from microSD card inserted on the BeagleBone board. We will discuss about this in detail in the Setting up your BeagleBone board and installing operating system's topics of this chapter.

BeagleBone Black – a single board computer

This topic will give you brief information about single board computers to make you understand what they are and where BeagleBone boards fit inside this category.

Have you ever wondered how your smartphones, smart TVs, and set-top boxes work?

All these devices run custom firmware developed for specific applications based on the different Linux and Unix kernels. When you hear the word Linux and if you are familiar with Linux, you will get in your mind that it's nothing but an operating system, just like Windows or Mac OS X that runs on desktops and server computers. But in the recent years the Linux kernel is being used in most of the embedded systems including consumer electronics such as your smartphones, smart TVs, set-top boxes, and much more. Most people know Android and iOS as an operating system on their smart phones. But only a few know that, both these operating systems are based on Linux and Unix kernels.

Did you ever question how they would develop such devices? There should be a development board right? What are they?

This is where Linux Development boards like our BeagleBone boards are used.

By adding peripherals such as touch screens, GSM modules, microphones, and speakers to these single board computers and writing the software that is the operating system with graphical user interface to make them interact with the physical world, we have so many smart devices now that people use every day.

Nowadays you have proximity sensors, accelerometers, gyroscopes, cameras, IR blasters, and much more on your smartphones. These sensors and transmitters are connected to the CPU on your phone through the Input Output ports on the CPU, and there is a small piece of software that is running to communicate with these electronics when the whole operating system is running in the smartphone to get the readings from these sensors in real-time. Like the autorotation of screen on the latest smartphones. There is a small piece of software that is reading the data from accelerometer and gyroscope sensors on the phone and based on the orientation of the phone it turns the graphical display.

So, all these Linux development boards are tools and base boards using which you can build awesome real world smart devices or we can call them physical computing systems as they interact with the physical world and respond with an output.

Getting to know your board – BeagleBone Black

BeagleBone Black can be described as low cost single board computer that can be plugged into a computer monitor or TV via a HDMI cable for output and uses standard keyboard and mouse for input. It's capable of doing everything you'd expect a desktop computer to do, like playing videos, word processing, browsing the Internet, and so on. You can even setup a web server on your BeagleBone Black just like you would do if you want to set up a webserver on a Linux or Windows PC.

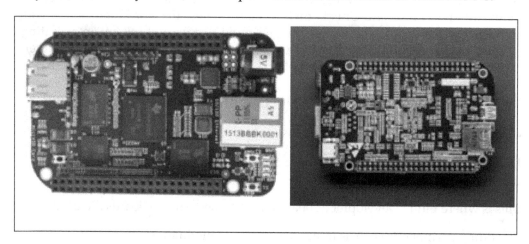

But, differing from your desktop computer, the BeagleBone boards has the ability to interact with the physical world using the GPIO pins available on the board, and has been used in various physical computing applications. Starting from Internet of Things, Home Automation projects, to Robotics, or tweeting shark intrusion systems. The BeagleBone boards are being used by hardware makers around the world to build awesome physical computing systems which are turning into commercial products also in the market. OpenROV, an underwater robot being one good example of what someone can build using a BeagleBone Black that can turn into a successful commercial product.

Hardware specification of BeagleBone Black

A picture is worth a thousand words. The following picture describes about the hardware specifications of the BeagleBone Black. But you will get some more details about every part of the board as you read the content in the following picture.

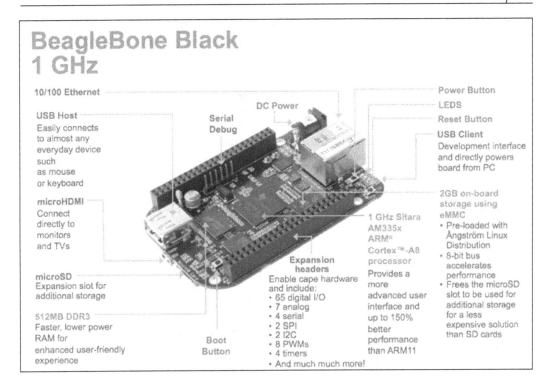

If you are familiar with the basic setup of a computer. You will know that it has a CPU with RAM and Hard Disk. To the CPU you can connect your Keyboard, Mouse, and Monitor which are powered up using a power system.

The same setup is here in BeagleBone Black also. There is a 1GHz Processor with 512MB of DDR3 RAM and 4GB on board eMMC storage, which replaces the Hard Disk to store the operating system. Just in case you want more storage to boot up using a different operating system, you can use an external microSD card that can have the operating system that you can insert into the microSD card slot for extra storage.

As in every computer, the board consists of a power button to turn on and turn off the board and a reset button to reset the board. In addition, there is a boot button which is used to boot the board when the operating system is loaded on the microSD card instead of the eMMC. We will be learning about usage of this button in detail in the installing operating systems topic of this chapter.

There is a type A USB Host port to which you can connect peripherals such as USB Keyboard, USB Mouse, USB Camera, and much more, provided that the Linux drivers are available for the peripherals you connect to the BeagleBone Black.

 It is to be noted that the BeagleBone Black has only one USB Host Port, so you need to get an USB Hub to get multiple USB ports for connecting more number of USB devices at a time. I would recommend using a wireless Keyboard and Mouse to eliminate an extra USB Hub when you connect your BeagleBone Black to monitor using the HDMI port available.

The microHDMI port available on the BeagleBone Black gives the board the ability to give output to HDMI monitors and HDMI TVs just like any computer will give.

You can power up the BeagleBone Black using the DC Barrel jack available on the left hand side corner of the board using a 5V DC, 2A adapter. There is an option to power the board using USB, although it is not recommended due to the current limit on USB ports. We will see about this in detail in the upcoming chapters when we connect USB Wi-Fi dongle and USB camera to the BeagleBone Black.

There are 4 LEDs on board to indicate the status of the board and help us for identifications to boot up the BeagleBone Black from microSD card. The LEDs are linked with the GPIO pins on the BeagleBone Black which can be used whenever needed.

You can connect the BeagleBone Black to the LAN or Internet using the Ethernet port available on the board using an Ethernet cable. You can even use a USB Wi-Fi module to give Internet access to your BeagleBone Black. In *Chapter 5, Connecting Physical Computing Systems to the Internet*, you will learn how to do this.

The expansion headers which are in general called the General Purpose Input Output (GPIO) pins include 65 digital pins. These pins can be used as digital input or output pins to which you can connect switches, LEDs and many more digital input output components, 7 analog inputs to which you can connect analog sensors like a potentiometer or an analog temperature sensor, 4 Serial Ports to which you can connect Serial Bluetooth or Xbee Modules for wireless communication or anything else, 2 SPI and 2 I2C Ports to connect different modules such as sensors or any other modules using SPI or I2C communication. It also has 8 PWM output pins that can be used for applications like fading and LED or in robotic applications for varying the speed of a motor which we will be discussing later in the upcoming chapters.

We also have the serial debugging port to view the low-level firmware pre-boot and post-shutdown/reboot messages via a serial monitor using an external serial to USB converter while the system is loading up and running. After booting up the operating system, this also acts as a fully interactive Linux console.

Setting up your BeagleBone board

Your first step to get started with BeagleBone boards with your hands on will be to set it up and test it as suggested by the BeagleBone Community with the Debian distribution of Linux running on BeagleBone Black that comes preloaded on the eMMC on board. This section will walk you through that process followed by installing different operating system on your BeagleBone board and log in into it. And then get into start working with files and executing Linux Shell commands via SSH.

1. Connect your BeagleBone Black using the USB cable to your Laptop or PC.

    This is the simplest method to get your BeagleBone Black up and running. Once you connect your BeagleBone Black, it will start to boot using the operating system on the eMMC storage. To log in into the operating system and start working on it, the BeagleBone Black has to connect to a network and the drivers that are provided by the BeagleBoard manufacturers allow us to create a local network between your BeagleBone Black and your computer when you connect it via the USB cable. For this, you need to download and install the device drivers provided by BeagleBone board makers on your PC as explained in step 2.

2. Download and install device drivers.

   ○ Goto `http://beagleboard.org/getting-started`

   ○ Click and download the driver package based on your operating system. Mine is Windows (64-bit), so I am going to download that

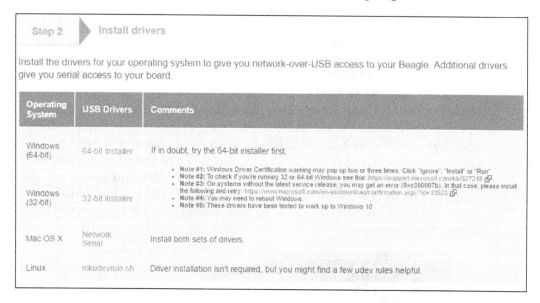

Once the installation is complete, click on **Finish**. It is shown in the following screenshot:

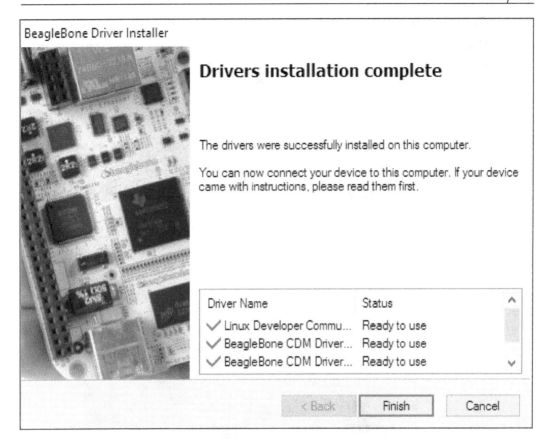

Once the installation is done, restart your PC. Make sure that the Wi-Fi on your laptop is off and also there is no Ethernet connected to your Laptop. Because now the BeagleBone Black device drivers will try to create a LAN connection between you laptop and BeagleBone Black so that you can access the webserver running by default on the BeagleBone Black to test it's all good, up, and running. Once you reboot your PC, get to step 3.

3. Connect to the Web Server Running on BeagleBone Black.

Open your favorite web browser and enter the IP address `192.168.7.2` on the URL bar, which is the default static IP assigned to BeagleBone Black. This should open up the webpage as shown in the following screenshot:

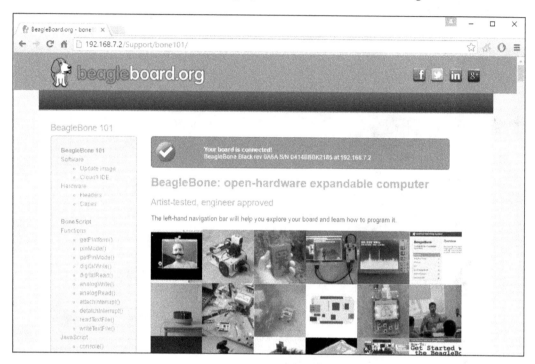

If you get a green check mark with the message your board is connected. You can make sure that you got the previous steps correct and you have successfully connected to your board.

If you don't get this message, try removing the USB cable connected to the BeagleBone Black, reconnect it and check again. If you still don't get it. Then check whether you did the first two steps correctly.

4. Play with on board LEDs via the web server.

If you Scroll down on the web page to which we got connected, you will find the section as shown in the following screenshot:

BoneScript interactive guide

BoneScript is a JavaScript library to simplify learning how to perform physical computing tasks using your embedded Linux. This web page is able to interact with your board to provide an interactive tutorial.

Example | run | restore

```
 1    var b = require('bonescript');
 2    b.pinMode('USR0', b.OUTPUT);
 3    b.pinMode('USR1', b.OUTPUT);
 4    b.pinMode('USR2', b.OUTPUT);
 5    b.pinMode('USR3', b.OUTPUT);
 6    b.digitalWrite('USR0', b.HIGH);
 7    b.digitalWrite('USR1', b.HIGH);
 8    b.digitalWrite('USR2', b.HIGH);
 9    b.digitalWrite('USR3', b.HIGH);
10    setTimeout(restore, 2000);
11    |
```

This is a sample setup made by BeagleBone makers as the first time interaction interface to make you understand what is possible using BeagleBone Black. In this section of the webpage, you can run a small script. When you click on **Run**, the On board status LEDs that are flashing depending on the status of the operating system will stop its function and start working based on the script that you see on the page. The code is running based on a JavaScript library built by BeagleBone makers called the **BoneScript**. We will not look into this in detail as we will be concentrating more on writing our own programs using python to work with GPIOs on the board. But to make you understand, here is a simple explanation on what is there on the script and what happens when you click on the run button on the webpage.

The `pinMode` function defines the on board LED pins as outputs and the `digitalWrite` function sets the state of the output either as HIGH or LOW. And the `setTimeout` function will restore the LEDs back to its normal function after the set timeout, that is, the program will stop running after the time that was set in the `setTimeout` function.

Say I modify the code to what is shown in the following screenshot:

BoneScript interactive guide

BoneScript is a JavaScript library to simplify learning how to perform physical computing tasks using your embedded Linux. This web page is able to interact with your board to provide an interactive tutorial.

Example `run` `restore`

```
1   var b = require('bonescript');
2   b.pinMode('USR0', b.OUTPUT);
3   b.pinMode('USR1', b.OUTPUT);
4   b.pinMode('USR2', b.OUTPUT);
5   b.pinMode('USR3', b.OUTPUT);
6   b.digitalWrite('USR0', b.HIGH);
7   b.digitalWrite('USR1', b.LOW);
8   b.digitalWrite('USR2', b.LOW);
9   b.digitalWrite('USR3', b.HIGH);
10  setTimeout(restore, 10000);
11
```

 You can notice that, I have changed the states of two LEDs to LOW and other two are HIGH and the timeout is set to 10,000 milliseconds.

So when you click on the Run button. The LEDs will switch to these states and stay like that for 10 seconds and then restore back to its normal status indication routine, that is, blinking.

You can play around with different combinations of HIGH and LOW states and setTimeout values so that you can see and understand what is happening.

You can see the LED output state of BeagleBone Black in the following screenshot for the program we executed earlier:

You can see that the two LEDs in the middle are in LOW state. It stays like this for 10 seconds when you run the script and then it will restore back to its usual routine. You can try with different timeout values and states of LEDs on the script given in the webpage and try clicking on the Run button to see how it works.

Like this we will be writing our own python programs and setting up servers to use the GPIOs available on the BeagleBone Black to make them work the way we desire to build different applications in each project that is available in this book.

Installing operating systems

We can make the BeagleBone Black boot up and run using different operating systems just like any computer can do. Mostly Linux is used on these boards which is free and open source, but it is to be noted that specific distributions of Linux, Android, and Windows CE have been made available for these boards as well which you can try out.

The stable versions of these operating systems are made available at http://beagleboard.org/latest-images.

By default, the BeagleBone Black comes preloaded with a Debian distribution of Linux on the eMMC of the board. However, if you want, you can flash this eMMC just like you do to your Hard Drive on your computer and install different operating systems on it.

As mentioned in the note at the beginning of this chapter, considering all the tutorials in this book should be useful to people who own BeagleBone as well as the BeagleBone Black. We will choose the recommended Debian package by www.BeagleBoard.org Foundation and we will boot the board every time using the operating system on microSD card.

Perform the following steps to prepare the microSD card and boot BeagleBone using that:

1. Goto: `http://beagleboard.org/latest-images`.

2. Download the latest Debian Image.

   The following screenshot highlights the latest Debian Image available for flashing on microSD card:

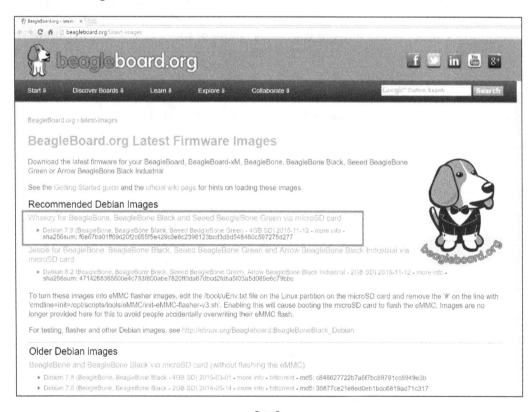

3. Extract the image file inside the RAR file that was downloaded:

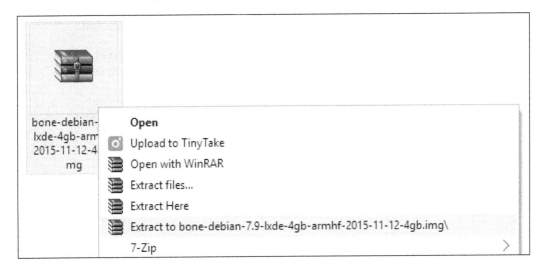

 You might have to install WinRAR or any `.rar` file extracting software if it is not available in your computer already.

4. Install Win32 Disk Imager software.

    To write the image file to a microSD card, we need this software. You can go to Google or any other search engine and type `win32 disk imager` as keyword and search to get the web link to download this software as shown in the following screenshot:

The web link, where you can find this software is `http://sourceforge.net/projects/win32diskimager/`. But this keeps changing often that's why I suggest you can search it via any search engine with the keyword.

5. Once you download the software and install it. You should be able to see the window as shown in the following screenshot when you open the Win32 Disk Imager:

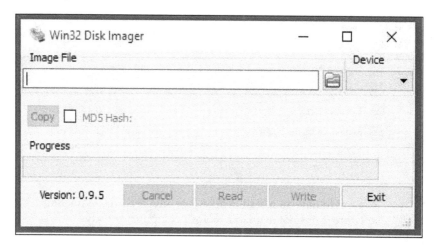

Now that you are all set with the software, using which you can flash the operating system image that we downloaded. Let's move to the next step where you can use Win32 Disk Imager software to flash the microSD card.

6. Flashing the microSD card.

    Insert the microSD into a microSD card reader and plug it onto your computer. It might take some time for the card reader to show up your microSD card. Once it shows up, you should be able to select the USB drive as shown in the following screenshot on the Win32 Disk Imager software.

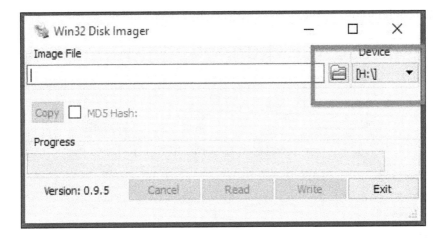

7. Now, click on the icon highlighted in the following screenshot to open the file explorer and select the image file that we extracted in step 3:

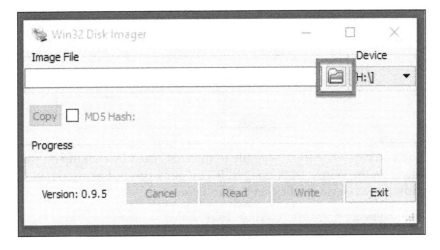

8. Go to the folder where you extracted the latest Debian image file and select it.

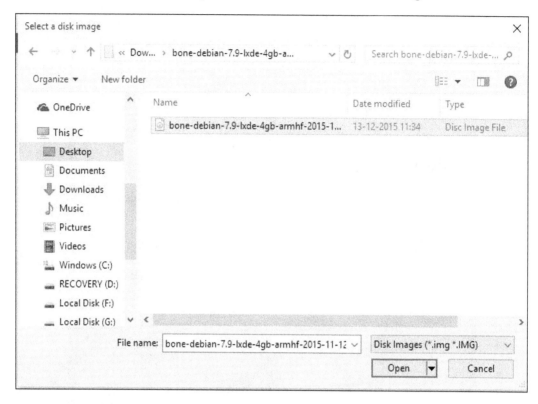

9. Now you can write the image file to microSD card by clicking on the **Write** button on the Win32 Disk Imager. If you get a prompt as shown in the following screenshot, click on **Yes** and continue:

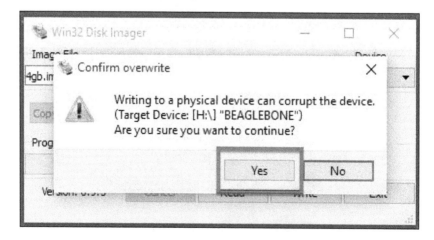

10. Once you click on **Yes**, the flashing process will start and the image file
    will be written on to the microSD card. The following screenshot shows
    the flashing process progressing:

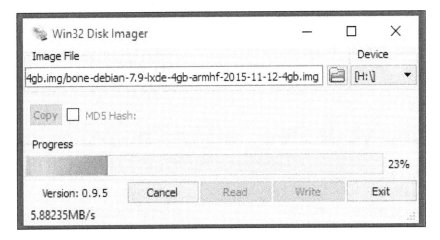

Once the flashing is completed, you will get a message as shown in the
following screenshot:

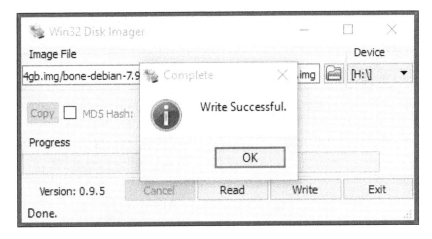

11. Now you can click on **OK**, exit the Win32 Disk Imager software and safely
    remove the microSD card from your computer.

Now you have successfully prepared your microSD card with the latest Debian operating system available for BeagleBone Black. This process is same for all other operating systems that are available for BeagleBone boards. You can try out different operating systems such as the Angstrom Linux, Android, or Windows CE others, once you get familiar with your BeagleBone board by end of this book.

For Mac users, you can refer to either `https://learn.adafruit.com/ssh-to-beaglebone-black-over-usb/installing-drivers-mac` or `https://learn.adafruit.com/beaglebone-black-installing-operating-systems/mac-os-x`.

Booting your BeagleBone board from a SD card

Since you have the operating system on your microSD card now, let us go ahead and boot your BeagleBone board from that microSD card and see how to login and access the filesystem via Linux Shell.

You will need your computer connected to your Router either via Ethernet or Wi-Fi and an Ethernet cable which you should connect between your Router and the BeagleBone board. The last but most important thing is an External Power Supply using which you will power up your BeagleBone board because power supply via a USB will be not be enough to run the BeagleBone board when it is booted from a microSD card.

1. Insert the microSD card into BeagleBone board.

    Now you should insert the microSD card that you have prepared into the microSD card slot available on your BeagleBone board.

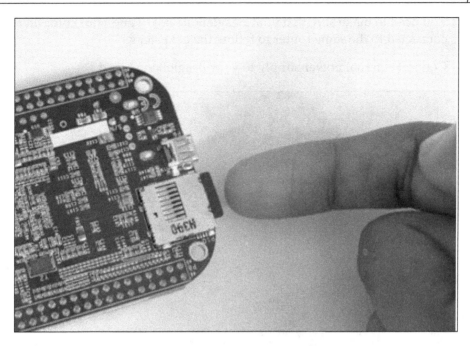

2. Connect your BeagleBone to your LAN.

   Now connect your BeagleBone board to your Internet router using an Ethernet cable.

You need to make sure that your BeagleBone board and your computer are connected to the same router to follow the next steps.

3. Connect external power supply to your BeagleBone board.

4. Boot your BeagleBone board from microSD card.

On BeagleBone Black and BeagleBone Green, you have a Boot Button which you need to hold on while turning on your BeagleBone board so that it starts booting from the microSD card instead of the default mode where it starts to boot from the onboard eMMC storage which holds the operating system. In case of BeagleBone White, you don't have this button, it starts to boot from the microSD card itself as it doesn't have onboard eMMC storage.

Depending on the board that you have, you can decide whether to boot the board from microSD card or eMMC. Consider you have a BeagleBone Black just like the one I have shown in the preceding picture. You hold down the User Boot button that is highlighted on the image and turn on the power supply. Once you turn on the board while holding the button down, the four on-board LEDs will light up and stay HIGH as shown in the following picture for 1 or 2 seconds, then they will start to blink randomly.

Once they start blinking, you can leave the button.

Now your BeagleBone board must have started Booting from the microSD card, so our next step will be to log in to the system and start working on it. The next topic will walk you through the steps on how to do this.

Logging into the board via SSH over Ethernet

If you are familiar with Linux operations, then you might have guessed what this section is about. But for those people who are not daily Linux users or have never heard the term SSH, **Secure Shell (SSH)** is a network protocol that allows network services and remote login to be able to operate over an unsecured network in a secure manner. In basic terms, it's a protocol through which you can log in to a computer and assess its filesystem and also work on that system using specific commands to create and work with files on the system.

In the steps ahead, you will work with some Linux commands that will make you understand this method of logging into a system and working on it.

1. Setup SSH Software.

   To get started, log in to your BeagleBone board now, from a Windows PC, you need to install any SSH terminal software for Windows.

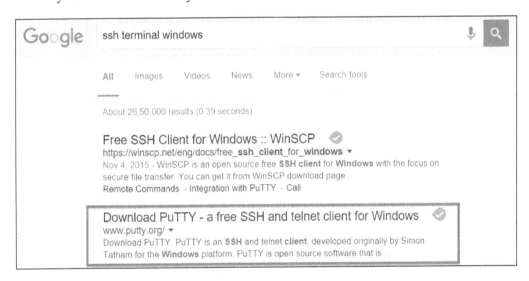

My favorite is PuTTY, so I will be using that in the steps ahead. If you are new to using SSH, I would suggest you also get PuTTY.

The software interface of PuTTY will be as shown in the following screenshot:

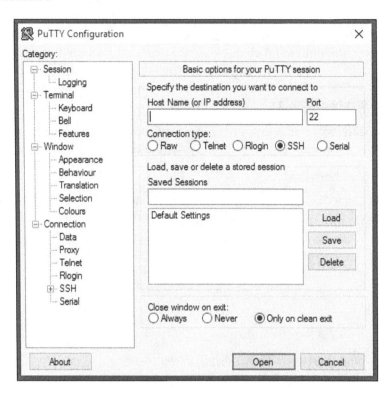

You need to know the IP address or the Host Name of your BeagleBone Black to log in to it via SSH. The default Host Name is beaglebone but in some routers, depending on their security settings, this method of login doesn't work with Host Name. So, I would suggest you try to login entering the hostname first. If you are not able to login, follow step 2. If you successfully connect and get the login prompt with Host Name, you can skip step 2 and go to Step 3.

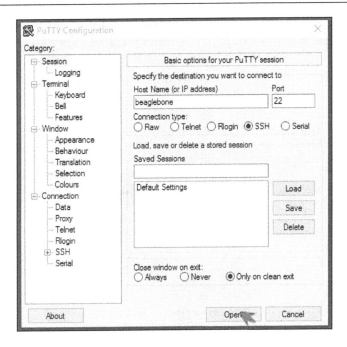

But if you get an error as shown in the following screenshot, perform Step 2.

2. Find an IP address assigned to BeagleBone board.

   Whenever you connect a device to your Router, say your computer, printer, or mobile phone. The router assigns a unique IP to these devices. The same way, the router must have assigned an IP to your BeagleBone board also. We can get this detail on the router's configuration page of your router from any browser of a computer that is connected to that router.

In most cases, the router can be assessed by entering the IP 192.168.1.1 but some router manufacturers have a different IP in very rare cases. If you are not able to assess your router using this IP 192.168.1.1, refer your router manual for getting access to this page.

The images that are shown in this section are to give you an idea about how to log in to your router and get the IP address details assigned to your BeagleBone board from your router. The configuration pages and how the devices are shown on the router will look different depending on the router that you own.

Enter the 192.168.1.1 address in you browser.

When it asks for **User Name** and **Password**, enter admin as **User Name** and password as **Password**

These are the mostly used credentials by default in most of the routers. Just in case you fail in this step, check your router's user manual.

Considering you logged into your router configuration page successfully, you will see the screen with details as shown in the following screenshot:

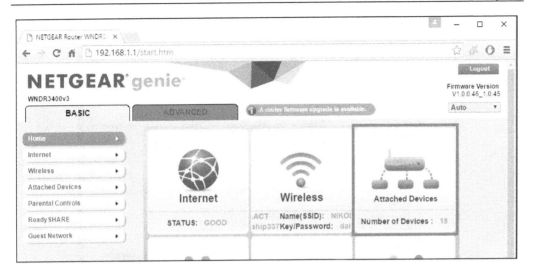

If you click on the highlighted part, **Attached Devices**, you will be able to see the list of devices with their IP as shown in the following screenshot, where you can find the details of the IP address that is assigned to your BeagleBone board.

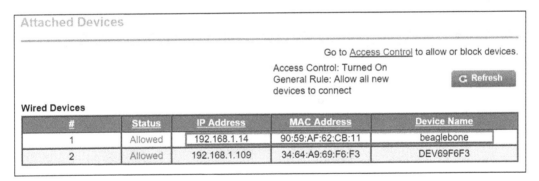

So now you can note down the IP that has been assigned to your BeagleBone board. It can be seen that it's `192.168.1.14` in the preceding screenshot for my beaglebone board. We will be using this IP address to connect to the BeagleBone board via SSH in the next step.

3. Connect via SSH using IP Address.

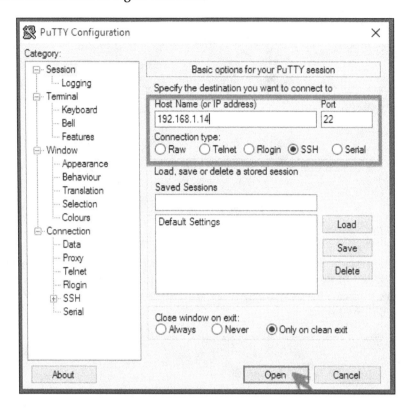

Once you click on **Open** you might get a security prompt as shown in the following screenshot. Click on **Yes** and continue.

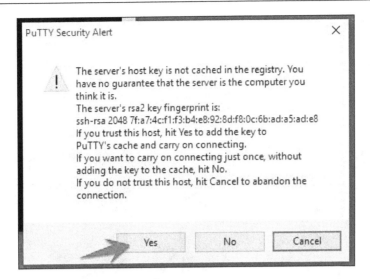

Now you will get the login prompt on the terminal screen as shown in the following screenshot:

If you got this far successfully, then it is time to log in to your BeagleBone board and start working on it via Linux Shell.

4. Log in to BeagleBone board.

    When you get the login prompt as shown in the preceding screenshot, you
    need to enter the default username which is debian and default password
    which is temppwd. Now you should have logged into Linux Shell of your
    BeagleBone board as user with username debian.

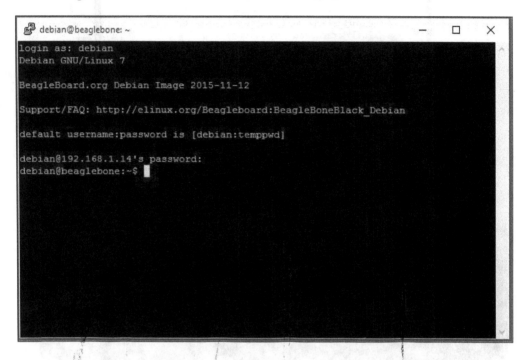

Now that you have successfully logged into your BeagleBone board's Linux Shell,
you can start working on it using Linux Shell commands like anyone does on any
computer that is running Linux.

The next section will walk you through some basic Linux Shell commands that will
come in handy for you to work with any Linux system.

Working on Linux Shell

Simply put, the shell is a program that takes commands from the keyboard and gives them to the operating system to perform. Since we will be working on BeagleBone board as a development board to build electronics projects, plugging it to a Monitor, Keyboard, and Mouse every time to work on it like a computer might be unwanted most of the times and you might need more resources also which is unnecessary all the time. So we will be using the shell command-line interface to work on the BeagleBone boards. If you want to learn more about the Linux command-line interfaces, I would suggest you visit to `http://linuxcommand.org/`.

Now let's go ahead and try some basic shell commands and do something on your BeagleBone board.

You can see the kernel version using the command `uname -r`. Just type the command and hit enter on your keyboard, the command will get executed and you will see the output as shown here:

```
debian@beaglebone:~$ uname -r
3.8.13-bone79
```

Next, let us check the `date` on your BeagleBone board:

```
debian@beaglebone:~$ date
Sun Dec 13 12:45:26 UTC 2015
```

Like this shell will execute your commands and you can work on your BeagleBone boards via the shell.

Getting kernel version and date was just for a sample test. Now let's move ahead and start working with the filesystem.

- `ls`: This stands for list command. This command will list out and display the names of folders and files available in the current working directory on which you are working.

```
debian@beaglebone:~$ ls
Desktop  bin
```

- pwd: This stands for print working directory command. This command prints the current working directory in which you are present.

```
debian@beaglebone:~$ pwd
/home/debian
```

- mkdir: This stands for make directory command. This command will create a directory in other words a folder, but you need to mention the name of the directory you want to create in the command followed by it.

Say I want to create a folder with the name WorkSpace, I should enter the command as follows:

```
debian@beaglebone:~$ mkdir WorkSpace
```

When you execute this command, it will create a folder named WorkSpace inside the current working directory you are in, to check whether the directory was created. You can try the ls command again and see that the directory named WorkSpace has been created.

```
debian@beaglebone:~$ ls
Desktop  WorkSpace  bin
```

To change the working directory and go inside the WorkSpace directory, you can use the next command that we will be seeing.

- cd: This stands for change directory command. This command will help you switch between directories depending on the path you provide along with this command.

Now to switch and get inside the WorkSpace directory that you created, you can type the command as follows:

```
cd WorkSpace
```

You can note that whenever you type a command, it executes in the current working that you are in. So the execution of cd WorkSpace now will be equivalent to cd /home/debian/WorkSpace as your current working directory is /home/debian.

```
debian@beaglebone:~$ cd WorkSpace
debian@beaglebone:~/WorkSpace$ []
```

Now you can see that you have got inside the `WorkSpace` folder, which is empty right now, so if you type the `ls` command now, it will just go to the next line on the shell terminal, it will not output anything as the folder is empty.

```
debian@beaglebone:~/WorkSpace$ ls
debian@beaglebone:~/WorkSpace$ []
```

Now if you execute the `pwd` command, you will see that your current working directory has changed.

```
debian@beaglebone:~/WorkSpace$ pwd
/home/debian/WorkSpace
```

- `cat`: This stands for the cat command. This is one of the most basic commands that is used to read, write, and append data to files in shell.

To create a text file and add some content to it, you just need to type the `cat` command `cat > filename.txt`

Say I want to create a sample.txt file, I would type the command as shown next:

```
debian@beaglebone:~/WorkSpace$ cat > sample.txt
▮
```

Once you type, the cursor will be waiting for the text you want to type inside the text file you created. Now you can type whatever text you want to type and when you are done press *Ctrl + D*. It will save the file and get back to the command-line interface.

Say I typed **This is a test** and then pressed *Ctrl + D*. The shell will look as shown next.

```
debian@beaglebone:~/WorkSpace$ cat > sample.txt
This is a test
```

Now if you type `ls` command, you can see the text file inside the `WorkSpace` directory.

```
debian@beaglebone:~/WorkSpace$ ls
sample.txt
```

If you want to read the contents of the `sample.txt` file, again you can use the `cat` command as follows:

```
debian@beaglebone:~/WorkSpace$ cat sample.txt
This is a test
```

Alternatively, you can even use the `more` command which we will be using mostly:

```
debian@beaglebone:~/WorkSpace$ more sample.txt
This is a test
```

Now that we saw how we can create a file, let's see how to delete what we created.

- `rm`: This stands for remove command. This will let you delete any file by typing the filename or filename along with path followed by the command.

Say now we want to delete the `sample.txt` file we created, the command can be either `rm sample.txt` which will be equivalent to `rm /home/debian/WorkSpace/sample.txt` as your current working directory is `/home/debian/Workspace`.

```
debian@beaglebone:~/WorkSpace$ rm sample.txt
```

After you execute this command, if you try to list the contents of the directory, you will notice that the file has been deleted and now the directory is empty.

```
debian@beaglebone:~/WorkSpace$ ls
debian@beaglebone:~/WorkSpace$ []
```

Like this, you can make use of the shell commands work on your BeagleBone board via SSH over Ethernet or Wi-Fi. We will be seeing how to connect your BeagleBone board to Wi-Fi in *Chapter 5, Connecting Physical Computing Systems to the Internet* where you can setup your BeagleBone board to connect to your router via Wi-Fi instead of Ethernet to give wireless access to your BeagleBone board.

Now that you have got a clear idea and hands-on experience on using the Linux Shell, let's go ahead and start working with python and write a sample program on a text editor on Linux and test it in the next and last topic of this chapter.

Writing your own Python program on BeagleBone board

In this section, we will write our first few Python codes on your BeagleBone board. That will take an input and make a decision based on the input and print out an output depending on the code that we write. There are three sample codes in this topic as examples, which will help you cover some fundamentals of any programming language, including defining variables, using arithmetic operators, taking input and printing output, loops and decision making algorithm.

Before we write and execute a python program, let us get into python's interactive shell interface via the Linux shell and try some basic things like creating a variable and performing math operations on those variables.

To open the python shell interface, you just have the type python on the Linux shell like you did for any Linux shell command in the previous section of this chapter.

Once you type `python` and hit *Enter*, you should be able to see the terminal as shown in the following screenshot:

```
debian@beaglebone:~/WorkSpace$ python
Python 2.7.3 (default, Mar 14 2014, 17:55:54)
[GCC 4.6.3] on linux2
Type "help", "copyright", "credits" or "license" for more information.
>>> []
```

Now you are into python's interactive shell interface where every line that you type is the code that you are writing and executing simultaneously in every step. To learn more about this, visit `https://www.python.org/shell/` or to get started and learn python programming language you can get our *Python By Example* book in our publication.

Let's execute a series of syntax in python's interactive shell interface to see whether it's working.

Let's create a variable A and assign value 20 to it:

```
>>> A = 20
```

Now let's `print` A to check what value it is assigned:

```
>>> print A
20
```

You can see that it prints out the value that we stored on it.

Now let's create another variable named B and store value 30 to it:

```
>>> B = 30
```

Let's try adding these two variables and store the result in another variable named C. Then `print` C where you can see the result of *A+B*, that is, 50.

```
>>> C = B + A
>>> print C
50
```

That is the very basic calculation we performed on a programming interface. We created two variables with different values and then performed an arithmetic operation of adding two values on those variables and printed out the result.

Now, let's get a little more ahead and store string of characters in a variable and print them.

```
>>> D = "This is a sentence"
>>> print D
This is a sentence
```

Wasn't that simple. Like this you can play around with python's interactive shell interface to learn coding. But any programmer would like to write a code and execute the program to get the output on a single command right.

Let's see how that can be done now.

To get out of the Python's Interactive Shell and get back to the current working directory on Linux Shell, just hold the *Ctrl* button and press *D*, that is, *Ctrl + D* on the keyboard. You will be back on the Linux Shell interface as shown next:

```
debian@beaglebone:~/WorkSpace$ python
Python 2.7.3 (default, Mar 14 2014, 17:55:54)
[GCC 4.6.3] on linux2
Type "help", "copyright", "credits" or "license" for more information.
>>> A = 20
>>> print A
20
>>> B = 30
>>> C = B + A
>>> print C
50
>>> D = "This is a sentence"
>>> print D
This is a sentence
>>>
debian@beaglebone:~/WorkSpace$ []
```

Now let's go ahead and write the program to perform the same action that we tried executing on python's interactive shell. That is to store two values on different variables and print out the result when both of them are added. Let's add some spice to it by doing multiple arithmetic operations on the variables that we create and print out the values of addition and subtraction.

You will need a text editor to write programs and save them. You can do it using the cat command also. But in future when you use indentation and more editing on the programs, the basic cat command usage will be difficult. So, let's start using the available text editor on Linux named nano, which is one of my favorite text editors in Linux. If you have a different choice and you are familiar with other text editors on Linux, such as vi or anything else, you can go ahead and continue the next steps using them to write programs.

To create a python file and start writing the code on it using nano, you need to use the nano command followed by the filename with extension .py.

Let's create a file named ArithmeticOperations.py.

```
debian@beaglebone:~/WorkSpace$ nano ArithmeticOperations.py[]
```

Once you type this command, the text editor will open up.

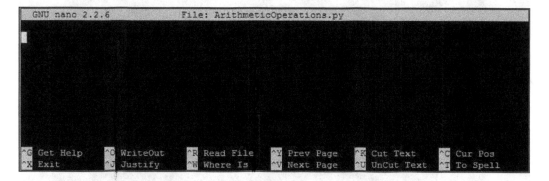

Here you can type your code and save it using the keyboard command *Ctrl + X*.

Let's go ahead and write the code which is shown in the following screenshot and let's save the file using *Ctrl + X*:

```
  GNU nano 2.2.6                    File: ArithmeticOperations.py

A = 20
B = 30
C = B + A
D = B - A
print "A + B is", C
print "A - B is", D



                                    [ Read 6 lines ]
^G Get Help        ^O WriteOut      ^R Read File     ^Y Prev Page     ^K Cut Text      ^C Cur Pos
^X Exit            ^J Justify       ^W Where Is      ^V Next Page     ^U UnCut Text    ^T To Spell
```

Then type *Y* when it prompts to save the modified file.

```
  GNU nano 2.2.6                    File: ArithmeticOperations.py                              Modified

A = 20
B = 30
C = B + A
D = B - A
print "A + B is", C
print "A - B is", D



Save modified buffer (ANSWERING "No" WILL DESTROY CHANGES) ?
 Y Yes
 N No              ^C Cancel
```

Then if you want to change the file with a different name, you can change it in the next step before you save it. Since we created the file now only, we don't need to do it. In case if you want to save the modified copy of the file in future with a different name, you can change the filename in this step:

```
  GNU nano 2.2.6              File: ArithmeticOperations.py                    Modified

A = 20
B = 30
C = B + A
D = B - A
print "A + B is", C
print "A - B is", D



File Name to Write: ArithmeticOperations.py
^G Get Help          M-D DOS Format         M-A Append              M-B Backup File
^C Cancel            M-M Mac Format         M-P Prepend
```

For now we will just hit *Enter* that will take us back to the Linux Shell and the file `AritmeticOperations.py` will be created inside the current working directory, which you can see by typing the `ls` command. You can also see the contents of the file by typing the `more` command that we learned in the previous section of this chapter.

```
debian@beaglebone:~/WorkSpace$ ls
ArithmeticOperations.py
debian@beaglebone:~/WorkSpace$ more ArithmeticOperations.py
A = 20
B = 30
C = B + A
D = B - A
print "A + B is", C
print "A - B is", D
debian@beaglebone:~/WorkSpace$ ▯
```

Now let's execute the python script and see the output. To do this, you just have to type the command python followed by the python program file that we created, that is, the `ArithmeticOperations.py`.

```
debian@beaglebone:~/WorkSpace$ python ArithmeticOperations.py
A + B is 50
A - B is 10
```

Once you run the python code that you wrote, you will see the output as shown earlier with the results as output.

Now that you have written and executed your first code on python and tested it working on your BeagleBone board, let's write another python code, which is shown in the following screenshot where the code will ask you to enter an input and whatever text you type as input will be printed on the next line and the program will run continuously.

Let's save this python code as `InputPrinter.py`:

```
GNU nano 2.2.6                    File: InputPrinter.py                         Modified

while True:
        name = raw_input("Enter Input: ")
        print name



^G Get Help    ^O WriteOut    ^R Read File   ^Y Prev Page   ^K Cut Text    ^C Cur Pos
^X Exit        ^J Justify     ^W Where Is    ^V Next Page   ^U UnCut Text  ^T To Spell
```

In this code, we will use a while loop so that the program runs continuously until you break it using the *Ctrl + D* command where it will break the program with an error and get back to Linux Shell.

```
debian@beaglebone:~/WorkSpace$ python InputPrinter.py
Enter Input: Jayakarthigeyan
Jayakarthigeyan
Enter Input: Hello
Hello
Enter Input: How are you
How are you
Enter Input: Traceback (most recent call last):
  File "InputPrinter.py", line 2, in <module>
    name = raw_input("Enter Input: ")
EOFError
debian@beaglebone:~/WorkSpace$
```

Now let's try out our third and last program of this section and chapter, where when we run the code, the program asks the user to type the user's name as input and if they type a specific name that we compare, it prints and says **Hello** message or if a different name was given as input, it prints **Go Away**; let's call this code `Say_Hello_To_Boss.py`.

```
GNU nano 2.2.6                    File: Say Hello To Boss.py                     Modified

while True:
        name = raw_input("What is your name? ")
        if name == "Jayakarthigeyan":
                print "Hello Boss"
        else:
                print "Go Away"




File Name to Write: Say Hello To Boss.py
^G Get Help    M-D DOS Format   M-A Append    M-B Backup File
^C Cancel      M-M Mac Format   M-P Prepend
```

Instead of my name **Jayakarthigeyan**, you can replace it with your name or any string of characters on comparing which, the output decision varies.

When you execute the code, the output will look as shown in the following screenshot:

```
debian@beaglebone:~/WorkSpace$ python Say_Hello_To_Boss.py
What is your name? Jayakarthigeyan
Hello Boss
What is your name? Jhon
Go Away
What is your name? Mark
Go Away
What is your name? Jayakarthigeyan
Hello Boss
What is your name? ^CTraceback (most recent call last):
  File "Say_Hello_To_Boss.py", line 2, in <module>
    name = raw_input("What is your name? ")
KeyboardInterrupt
debian@beaglebone:~/WorkSpace$ []
```

Like we did in the previous program, you can hit *Ctrl* + *D* to stop the program and get back to Linux Shell.

In this way, you can work with python programming language to create codes that can run on the BeagleBone boards in the way you desire.

Since we have come to the end of this chapter, let's give a break to our BeagleBone board.

Let's power off our BeagleBone board using the command `sudo poweroff`, which will shut down the operating system.

```
debian@beaglebone:~/WorkSpace$ sudo poweroff

Broadcast message from root@beaglebone (pts/0) (Sun Dec 13 16:00:50 2015):
The system is going down for system halt NOW!
debian@beaglebone:~/WorkSpace$ []
```

After you execute this command, if you get the error message shown in the following screenshot, it means the BeagleBoard has powered off.

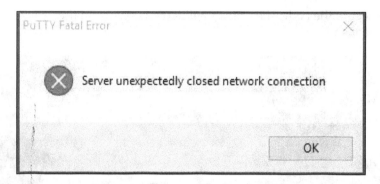

You can turn off the power supply that was connected to your BeagleBone board now.

Summary

So here we are at the end of this chapter. In this chapter, you have learned how to boot your BeagleBone board from a different operating system on microSD card and then log in to it and start coding in Python to run a routine and make decisions. Using this knowledge, we will see how to make an LED blink which is connected to any GPIO pin on the GPIO headers of the BeagleBone board and how to read the switch button status using python code in the next few chapters. But before that, we will look at fundamentals of Basic Electronics in the next chapter.

On an extra note, you can take this chapter to another level by trying out a little more by connecting your BeagleBone board to an HDMI monitor using a microHDMI cable and connecting a USB Keyboard and Mouse to the USB Host of the BeagleBone board and power the monitor and BeagleBone board using external power supply and boot it from microSD Card and you should be able to see some GUI and you will be able to use the BeagleBone board like a normal Linux computer. You will be able access the files, manage them, and use Shell Terminal on the GUI also. If you own BeagleBone Black or BeagleBone Green, you can try out to flash the onboard eMMC using the latest Debian operating system and try out the same thing that we did using the operating system booted from microSD card.

2
Circuit Fundamentals and GPIO

In this chapter, we will be learning the basics of setting up an external electronic circuit that you can interface with the BeagleBone board using the **general-purpose input/output** (**GPIO**) pins available on it. The chapter will focus on making the reader understand how to wire electronic circuits with an explanation of how they work followed by using the GPIOs available on the BeagleBone board for their operation.

For readers who are from an electronics background, most of what is covered in the first three topics will be familiar but still I suggest you skim through the topics to brush up the basics. Since the book is written in such a way that readers without prior knowledge of electronics also get to understand and work on the projects, these topics have to be included in the chapter.

The contents of the chapter are divided into the following topics:

- Prerequisites
- Fundamentals of electrical and electronic circuits
- Use of BreadBoards
- Switches and LEDs
- GPIOs
- Adding libraries to Python
- Using python to access GPIOs
- Simple project: Blinking an LED using a Python script

Prerequisites

This topic will cover what parts you need to get started with BeagleBone Black online. You can buy these parts from your favorite online store or from any of your local stores. individual electronic components such as resistors, transistors, LEDs, and so on are connected with a power source element such as a battery or other power supply source using conductive wires through which current flows through these electronic components, it forms an electronic circuit:

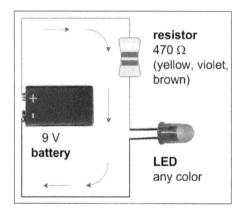

We will see how to make our first simple electric circuit using an LED followed by connecting a switch to it in the *Switches and LEDs* section of this chapter.

Usage of breadboards

In this section, you will learn about what breadboards are, why they are called so, and how to use them. Once you are done with it, you should have a basic understanding of how breadboards work and be able to start using it to build basic circuits on a breadboard.

A breadboard is composed of electrical connections in rows and columns. Each column is electrically connected to each point on the row, you can see the black column line, that has connectivity. You can use wires to connect any column with another. There are larger rows on the top and bottom which are usually used for power supply positive and negative, in other words, VCC (power) and GND (ground) signals. You can use these to easily connect any column to VCC or GND or use it for any other purpose as per your wish as there is no restriction, it's just like any other row:

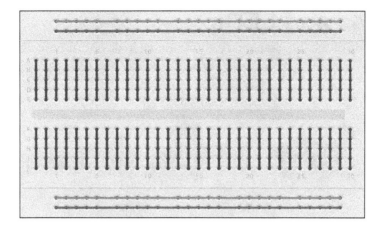

You can learn how to use a Breadboard by connecting the circuit given in the previous section to test it by setting up the same circuit on breadboard as shown in the following figure:

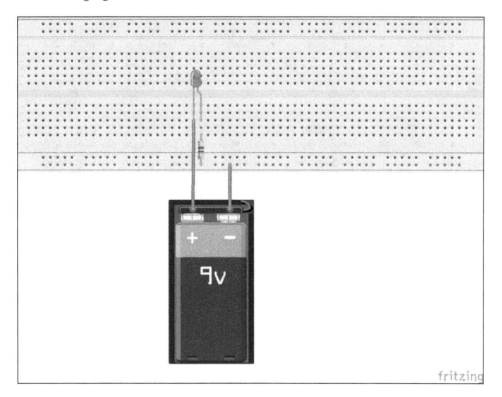

Switches and LEDs

Switches are one of the the elementary components in electronic circuits:

All they do is make or break a circuit, meaning it either opens a connection or closes it between two terminals. The two states of a switch are as shown in the following figure:

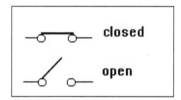

There are a lot of different types of switches. But there are two most commonly used ones in our circuits that we will discuss in this section, which are the momentary switch and the toggle switch. Before we discuss the different types of switches, as mentioned during the introduction of this chapter, let's see what LEDs are and how to create a basic circuit using them, as during the explanation of the switch operations, it will be useful for better understanding.

To create your first simple circuit, take a battery, resistor, and LED with wires to connect them as shown in the following figure. By doing this, you can understand what an LED is. LED stands for light emitting diode, which is nothing but an electronic component that emits light when suitable voltage is applied to its leads in the proper configuration. An LED has two leads: the cathode and the anode, as shown in the following figure:

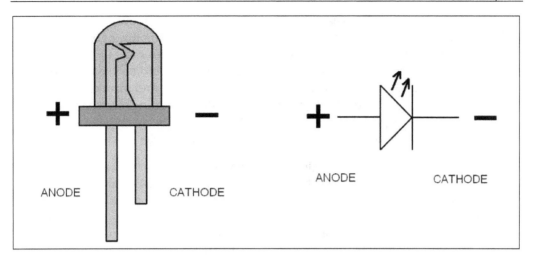

The anode terminal should be connected to the positive terminal of the power supply / battery and the cathode terminal should be connected to the negative terminal of the power supply / battery to make the LED glow. Connecting in reverse won't make the LED glow. If you would like to know more about why and how an LED works, do your research online or read books to find out more.

Now, let's go ahead and make an electronic circuit where current flows through the wires through a resistor and LED which are connected to a power source, in other words, a battery, as shown in the following diagram:

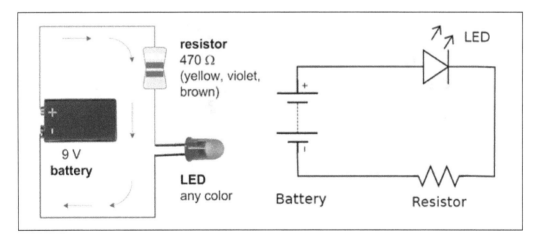

So, as shown in the preceding diagram, the resistor can be on any side of the LED. The resistor is a component that reduces the value of current flowing through the circuit. It is used to increase the lifetime of the LED and is necessary for most LEDs. I would suggest you learn more about how much value of resistor should be used and for particular battery and LEDs that you use because this chapter and most of the sections in it are intended to give you a basic getting started idea regarding electronic circuits. As mentioned at the beginning of the chapter, electrical and electronics is a vast topic and we can't put all the concepts involved in it in just one chapter.

If you successfully make the LED glow with a battery and LED with a resistor in between, you will have made your first basic electronic circuit. But have an LED glow all time is something that now one would want right. We will always need an element to control another element. So here comes the switch, where if you connect a switch in between this circuit, you can turn the LED on and off when you want it to glow or not glow. So let's go ahead and look at the two most-used types of switches in electronic circuits, which we will be using in the coming chapters to interface with the BeagleBone board to give inputs from the outside world.

Momentary switch

If you look at the following figure, you can see that the momentary switch has a push button actuator, a plunger in between the movable contact that touches the stationary contacts of two terminals.

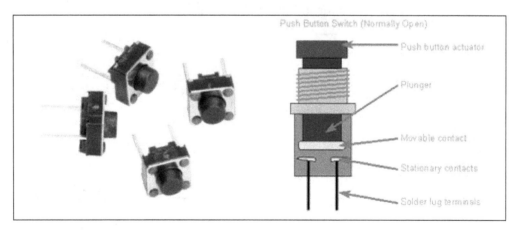

The switch shown in the preceding figure is normally open as the stationary contacts are not in contact with the movable contact during normal state as the plunger pulls the movable contact upwards. Whenever you press the button on top, the movable contact goes down and touches the two stationary terminals to make contact and close the line. When you remove the pressure you applied to press the push button switch, the plunger pulls back the movable contact and the circuit opens up. The explanation is illustrated in the following figure with an LED connected to a battery. Have a look at them to understand better and try it yourself using a push button momentary switch, a battery, a resistor, and an LED:

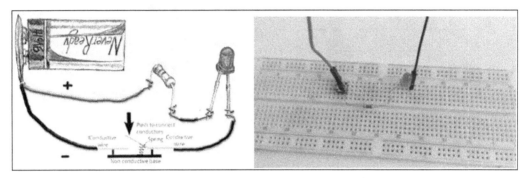

Pushbutton Open Circuit - No Current Flow so LED is OFF

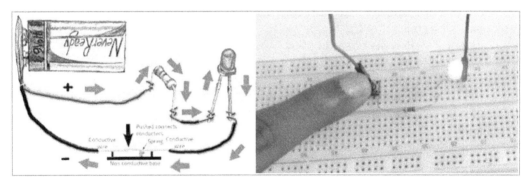

Pushbutton Closed Circuit - Current Flows so LED is ON

Please note that there are other types of push button momentary switches also available on the market which are normally closed, where the switch opens the circuit when the button is pressed and closes in normal state. Depending on which switch you use, the operation will differ for the circuit shown in the preceding figure. For normally closed, the LED will be always on and when you press the button, it will go off. For normally open, the operation will be as shown in the preceding figure, where the LED is off in normal state but goes on when you press the push button switch.

The next type of switch we will discuss will be the Toggle switch.

Toggle switch

A toggle switch is similar to the traditional switches used in wall-mounted electrical switch boards that help you open and close the connection to switch the circuit on and off. Here is how it looks with the circuit symbol:

Now that you are familiar with how a switch operation works, you can easily understand the concept of the toggle switch. Basically, it switches the state from on to off as we switch the position of the switch. Unlike the momentary switch, where we need to hold the switch button to switch the state, here, once you toggle the position, it stays in the position you left it. So we can toggle the switch from the Off to the On state, in other words, from the open to the closed state, as well as vice versa, and leave it as such and it will stay in the same position, in other words, in the state of either On or Off, as there is no spring mechanism to push the switch back to its previous position. The following diagrams will help you understand better:

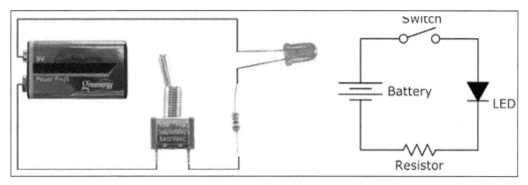

Toggle Switch Open Circuit - No Current Flow so LED is OFF

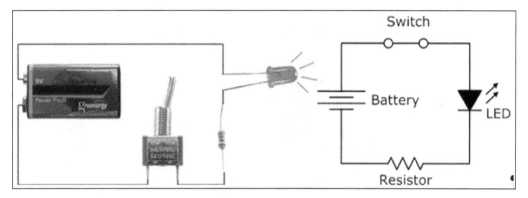

Toggle Switch Closed Circuit - Current Flows so LED is ON

So, as shown in the preceding figure, if you have successfully set up the circuit and made the LED glow by switching the switch, by now you must have understood the concept of an electrical circuit and switching an electrical and electronic circuit using a switch. But using our BeagleBone board instead of doing it manually, we will be using the GPIOs to switch elements as well as read the switching inputs. We will see this in detail with experiments in the next chapters. For now, in the next section, you will learn what GPIOs basically are and what kind of GPIOs are available on the BeagleBone board.

GPIOs

As we discussed in *Chapter 1, Getting Started with BeagleBone*, BeagleBone boards have GPIO pin headers on either side of the board. In this section, we will be discussing what these GPIOs are and how we can use them to interface external electronic components to the board.

The following figure shows the GPIOs available and the pin mapping of each of them. This pin mapping or, in general, the names assigned to these pins will be helpful for us while accessing them from the software running on the operating system. You will see this in detail at the end of the chapter, when we will be accessing the GPIO from python:

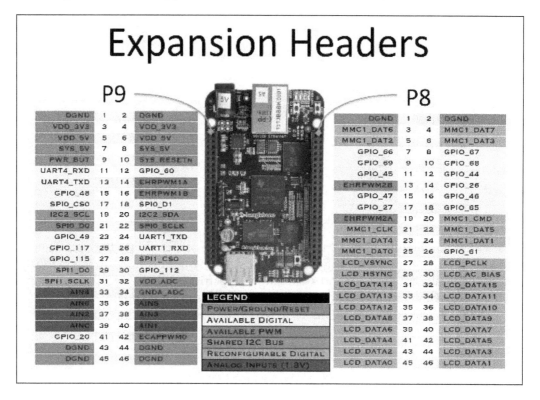

So, these GPIOs are ports which can act either as input or output from our definition from software running on the operating system. There are several methods to define these pins as input and output, as well as to change the state of these pins when defined as outputs and read the state when defined as inputs. In this book, as we will be using python as the primary programming language, we will be accessing these pins from the python program. To get started, you will first need to add a few libraries to python that will help you do it. How to install those libraries and validate them is explained in the next topic.

Adding libraries to Python

To make it easy to work with GPIOs on BeagleBone boards using Python programming language, we will be installing the `Adafruit-BeagleBone-IO-Python` library. The following steps will walk you through how to do it:

1. Log in to your BeagleBone board.

   As we did in the previous chapter, the first thing you need to do is boot the BeagleBone board from the microSD card and log in to it via SSH:

   ```
   login as: debian
   Debian GNU/Linux 7

   BeagleBoard.org Debian Image 2015-11-12

   Support/FAQ: http://elinux.org/Beagleboard:BeagleBoneBlack_Debian

   default username:password is [debian:temppwd]

   debian@192.168.1.15's password:
   Last login: Sun Jan 17 06:47:20 2016 from jay-tero.local
   debian@beaglebone:~$
   ```

2. Update the repositories.

   Your next step will be to update the software dependency repositories in Debian running on the BeagleBone board before we start installing the other dependencies that are not installed and the libraries.

You can use the `apt-get update` command to do this:

```
debian@beaglebone:~$ sudo apt-get update
Get:1 http://security.debian.org wheezy/updates Release.gpg [1554 B]
Get:2 http://ftp.us.debian.org wheezy Release.gpg [2373 B]
Get:3 http://security.debian.org wheezy/updates Release [102 kB]
Get:4 http://ftp.us.debian.org wheezy-updates Release.gpg [1554 B]
Get:5 http://ftp.us.debian.org wheezy Release [191 kB]
Get:6 http://repos.rcn-ee.com wheezy Release.gpg [819 B]
Get:7 http://security.debian.org wheezy/updates/main armhf Packages [404 kB]
Get:8 http://repos.rcn-ee.com wheezy Release [2172 B]
Get:9 http://repos.rcn-ee.com wheezy/main armhf Packages [229 kB]
Get:10 http://security.debian.org wheezy/updates/contrib armhf Packages [20 B]
Get:11 http://ftp.us.debian.org wheezy-updates Release [143 kB]
Get:12 http://security.debian.org wheezy/updates/non-free armhf Packages [20 B]
Get:13 http://ftp.us.debian.org wheezy/main armhf Packages [7444 kB]
Get:14 http://ftp.us.debian.org wheezy/contrib armhf Packages [39.3 kB]
Get:15 http://ftp.us.debian.org wheezy/non-free armhf Packages [67.8 kB]
Get:16 http://ftp.us.debian.org wheezy-updates/main armhf Packages [4857 B]
Get:17 http://ftp.us.debian.org wheezy-updates/contrib armhf Packages [20 B]
Get:18 http://ftp.us.debian.org wheezy-updates/non-free armhf Packages [20 B]
Fetched 8634 kB in 18s (477 kB/s)
Reading package lists... Done
debian@beaglebone:~$
```

3. Install the dependencies.

    In this step, we will be installing certain software packages that are necessary for the library to work with the BeagleBone board. The command that you need to execute is as follows:

    ```
    sudo apt-get install build-essential python-dev python-setuptools
    python-pip python-smbus -y
    ```

    The output that you will see is shown in the following screenshot:

```
debian@beaglebone:~$ sudo apt-get install build-essential python-dev python-setuptools python-pip python-smbus -y
Reading package lists... Done
Building dependency tree
Reading state information... Done
build-essential is already the newest version.
python-setuptools is already the newest version.
python-smbus is already the newest version.
python-pip is already the newest version.
The following NEW packages will be installed:
  python-dev
0 upgraded, 1 newly installed, 0 to remove and 0 not upgraded.
Need to get 920 B of archives.
After this operation, 25.6 kB of additional disk space will be used.
Get:1 http://ftp.us.debian.org/debian/ wheezy/main python-dev all 2.7.3-4+deb7u1 [920 B]
Fetched 920 B in 0s (1186 B/s)
Selecting previously unselected package python-dev.
(Reading database ... 60403 files and directories currently installed.)
Unpacking python-dev (from .../python-dev_2.7.3-4+deb7u1_all.deb) ...
Setting up python-dev (2.7.3-4+deb7u1) ...
debian@beaglebone:~$
```

4. Install the BBIO library.

   Now, once you have updated the repositories and installed the necessary dependencies, we can go ahead and install the `Adafruit_BBIO` Python Library that we will be using to access the GPIO pins on the BeagleBone board using Python running on it.

   To install the `Adafruit_BBIO` library, execute the following command:

   ```
   sudo pip install Adafruit_BBIO
   ```

   You will see the following output:

   ```
   debian@beaglebone:~$ sudo pip install Adafruit_BBIO
   Requirement already satisfied (use --upgrade to upgrade): Adafruit-BBIO in /usr/local/lib/python2.7/dist-packages
   Cleaning up...
   debian@beaglebone:~$
   ```

5. Test your installation.

   Now, let us check whether the installation happened properly or not. To do this, just execute the command given following:

   ```
   sudo python -c "import Adafruit_BBIO.GPIO as GPIO; print GPIO"
   ```

   Now, if you see the output shown in the following screenshot, it means the installation was successful and we have successfully installed the `Adafruit_BBIO` library:

   ```
   debian@beaglebone:~$ sudo python -c "import Adafruit_BBIO.GPIO as GPIO; print GPIO"
   <module 'Adafruit_BBIO.GPIO' from '/usr/local/lib/python2.7/dist-packages/Adafruit_BBIO/GPIO.so'>
   debian@beaglebone:~$
   ```

   We can validate this by importing the library into python and testing it, as shown in step 6.

6. Validate the installation.

   In this step, first you need to open Python's interactive shell to use the instructions, as shown following:

   ```
   debian@beaglebone:~$ sudo python
   Python 2.7.3 (default, Mar 14 2014, 17:55:54)
   [GCC 4.6.3] on linux2
   Type "help", "copyright", "credits" or "license" for more information.
   >>>
   >>> import Adafruit_BBIO.GPIO as GPIO
   >>> print GPIO
   <module 'Adafruit_BBIO.GPIO' from '/usr/local/lib/python2.7/dist-packages/Adafruit_BBIO/GPIO.so'>
   >>>
   ```

If you see the module available and its path when you print GPIO, it confirms that we have successfully installed and added the Adafruit_BBIO Library to Python. Now let's go ahead and access the GPIO from python to change its state from Python's interactive shell in the next section.

Using Python to access GPIOs

In this section, we will see how we can change the state of a GPIO on the BeagleBone board from python's interactive shell interface with the help of functions available in the Adafruit_BBIO Library.

You will have to connect an LED with one of the GPIO pins on the BeagleBone Black to understand how these GPIOs work. The following steps will walk you through the program that you can execute step by step on the Python's interactive shell interface to understand how you can change the state of a GPIO from LOW to HIGH and vice versa from python:

1. Connect an LED circuit to the BeagleBone board.

   To get started, we will need our Breadboard, LED, resistor, and hookup wires to connect the LED circuit with a GPIO available on the BeagleBone Black. Once you have them, connect the circuit as shown in the following figure:

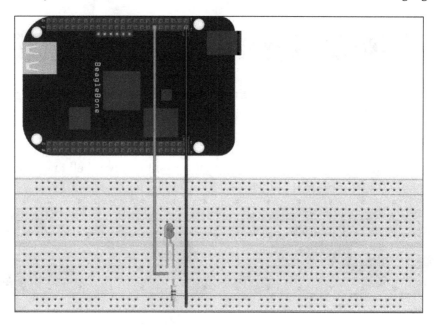

You can see that the cathode of the LED is connected to the Gnd pin on the BeagleBone Black through a 470-ohm resistor and the anode is connected to the GPIO pin 60 on the P9 header. You can refer to the expansion headers of BeagleBone Black for reference. Once you have connected the circuit with the BeagleBone Black, we can go ahead and start working with Python to make this LED turn on and off.

2. Open Python's interactive shell and import Adafruit's BBIO Library:

```
debian@beaglebone:~$ sudo python
Python 2.7.3 (default, Mar 14 2014, 17:55:54)
[GCC 4.6.3] on linux2
Type "help", "copyright", "credits" or "license" for more information.
>>> import Adafruit BBIO.GPIO as GPIO
```

As shown in the preceding screenshot, in this step, you will open Python's Interactive Shell and import the `Adafruit_BBIO` Module into it using the command shown in the preceding screenshot.

3. Set up pin GPIO_60 as OUTPUT.

Our next step will be to set up or define GPIO_60 as an output pin as we will be changing the state of the pin. You can note that these GPIO pins can be made to act as inputs or outputs. We will be seeing how they will be used as inputs in the next chapter. Right now we will be making this act as an output pin to change the state of the pin to high and low or vice versa, so we will define it as an output pin. To do this, the command is as follows:

```
GPIO.setup("P9_12", GPIO.OUT)
```

```
>>> GPIO.setup("P9 12", GPIO.OUT)
```

P9_12 is nothing but pin **GPIO_60**, which is the 12th pin on the P9 header. See the following figure to understand the idea behind the notation:

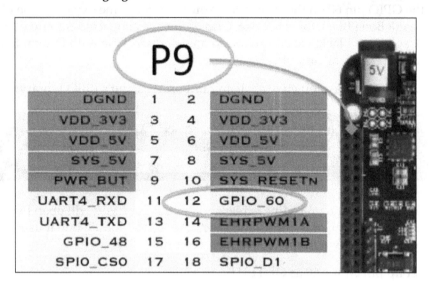

4. Set Pin GPIO_60 as HIGH.

Once we have defined the pin as an output pin, we can go ahead and change the state of the pin to HIGH or LOW. The function given following, when executed, will perform that operation:

```
GPIO.output("P9_12", GPIO.HIGH)
```

```
>>> GPIO.output("P9_12", GPIO.HIGH)
```

Now you will be able to see that the LED has turned on, as shown in the following image:

What exactly happens when you execute the function is one of the transistors inside the processor chip is turned on from the software and this makes GPIO_60 to HIGH state and it switches on and supplies 3.3V output, which makes the LED glow. You can now turn off the LED by setting the GPIO_60 pin to the LOW state, as shown in the next step, by modifying the GPIO. output function to LOW.

5. Set Pin GPIO_60 as LOW:

```
GPIO.output("P9_12", GPIO.LOW)
```

```
>>> GPIO.output("P9_12", GPIO.LOW)
```

Now you will be able to see that the LED has turned off, as shown in the following image:

As in the previous step, now the software turns off the transistor inside the microprocessor on the BeagleBone board to turn off the GPIO_60 so it turns off and becomes LOW, and doesn't give out the 3.3V supply so the LED is turned off.

6. Clean up the GPIO settings.

    So, now you will have got an idea that the GPIO states can be changed from the software running on the board. These GPIO pins stay in the previous state until they are changed to another state. But in situations where you stop the software in the middle of an operation, you might need the GPIO pins to go back to their default state, which is LOW for most of them. To do this, the Adafruit_BBIO library provides us with a function GPIO.cleanup(), which we will be using to clear the previous states and definitions of the GPIOs set from the software.

It is recommended that you use this function at the end of every program that you write, to avoid unnecessary, undesired output:

```
>>> GPIO.cleanup()
>>>
debian@beaglebone:~$ []
```

Project – blinking an LED using Python script

In the previous section, we saw how we can access the GPIO pin from Python's interactive shell and change its state. Let's now write a python code and save it as a .py file and run it like we did at the end of the previous chapter. The python program that is discussed in this section will make an LED blink at an interval of 1 second. The LED will be On for 1 second and Off for another 1 second; this will loop continuously until you break the loop.

The following screenshot shows the program:

```
GNU nano 2.2.6                 File: Blink.py

import time
import Adafruit_BBIO.GPIO as GPIO
GPIO.setup("P9_12", GPIO.OUT)
try:
    while True:
        print "Blinking"
        GPIO.output("P9_12", GPIO.HIGH)
        time.sleep(1)
        GPIO.output("P9_12", GPIO.LOW)
        time.sleep(1)

except KeyboardInterrupt:
    print "Keyboard Interrupt"
    GPIO.cleanup()
    print "GPIO Cleaned"[]

^G Get Help  ^O WriteOut  ^R Read Fil ^Y Prev Pag ^K Cut Text ^C Cur Pos
^X Exit      ^J Justify   ^W Where Is ^V Next Pag ^U UnCut Te ^T To Spell
```

The code imports the time module and the Adafruit_BBIO module just as we did in the interactive shell in the previous section of this chapter and then we set up GPIO_60 as an output pin and then changed the state of the pin to HIGH and LOW in the while loop that runs continuously. We use the time.sleep(1) function to pause the code for 1 second in between the state changes. The code also has the GPIO.clean() function that gets executed when a keyboard interrupt is given when the code is running.

To run the command, execute the following command after you save the code as a file called Blink.py:

```
sudo python Blink.py
```

You should see output as shown in the following screenshot and the LED connected to the BeagleBone board blinks at an interval of 1 second and the console also prints the text **Blinking**:

```
debian@beaglebone:~/WorkSpace$ sudo python Blink.py
Blinking
Blinking
Blinking
```

When you hit *Ctrl + C* to kill the program, it will clean up the GPIO to the default state and exit the program:

```
Blinking
Blinking
^CKeyboard Interrupt
GPIO Cleaned
debian@beaglebone:~/WorkSpace$
```

So, now you can go ahead and try to use different GPIOs and turn on and turn off the LED using decision-making statements and more from the Python program. If you remember, in *Chapter 1, Getting Started with BeagleBone*, we used the BoneScript library to make the LEDs which are on the board turn on and stay on for a timeout interval. You can try writing some code of that sort also in python and try keeping the LED on for some interval of time. And turn it off based on the input you will be giving.

Summary

Here we are at the end of this chapter, where we learnt the basic principle behind a simple electronic circuit using LEDs and switches. We saw what GPIOs are and how we can access them from python and wrote a simple code to make an LED blink at a particular interval. Then we added external libraries to python on BeagleBone boards. In the next chapter, we will be seeing how we can get an input from the external world and build a system that reacts to that input.

3
Introduction to Physical Computing Systems

This chapter will focus on giving you an introduction to what physical computing systems are, what they are composed of, how they work and where they are used. First, we will get started with a brief introduction to physical computing systems, which will give you a basic idea about the basic composition of physical computing systems with an example followed by its application areas, and at the end we will see how we can build our own physical computing system using BeagleBone Black with a push button and LED using Python programming to change the LED state based on the push button press input.

The contents of the chapter are divided into the following topics:

- Prerequisites
- Introduction to physical computing systems
- Basic elements of physical computing systems
- Application areas
- Simple project: Push button input triggers event on Python code to toggle LED on and off

Prerequisites

This topic will cover what parts you need in this chapter. These can be purchased from your favorite electrical hobby store or can simply be ordered online. We will need the following materials:

- 1 x BeagleBone Black
- 1 x microSD Card with latest version of Debian flashed on it to boot the BeagleBone board from the microSD Card
- 1 x 5V DC, 2A power supply
- 1 x Ethernet cable
- 1 x Breadboard
- 1 x push button switch
- 1 x LED
- 1 x 470-ohm resistor
- 1 x 4.7 Kilo ohm resistor

Introducing physical computing systems

This section will give you a basic overview of physical computing systems. Physical computing systems are electronic systems that use software and hardware together to get input from the physical world using the hardware and respond to it by providing an output based on the software running on the hardware. These systems are also called embedded systems in different applications. In general terms, any system that interacts with the analog world using hardware sensors and senses the input obtained and responds accordingly based on the software programmed for it is called a physical computing system.

Right from your music player, washing machine, automatic door opener, and mobile phone, everything that takes input from the physical world using sensors and buttons and responds to it by making a change in the physical world with its output is a physical computing system.

Take, for example, your washing machine. Based on the input you provide by clicking on the buttons available on it, which is a physical input from the world to the washing machine system, it washes your clothes and dries them, which is again an output on the physical world; it is changing the physical things, the clothes, using air and water. So it is basically creating a change in the physical, analog world with its output, which is based on the software running on the hardware on the washing machine system with the sensors and actuators available on it. We will look at this in detail with block diagrams and more examples with explanations in the next section of this chapter, which looks at the basic components comprising a physical computing system and how they work.

Basic elements of physical computing systems

In this section, you will learn what physical computing systems are composed of. First, we will see the basic structure of input and output elements and how to act and react, followed by the structure of it based on the electrical, electronic, and software aspects, including the input and output of the system. At the end, we will try to get a much clearer picture of the same concepts with examples.

The basic structure of a physical computing system comprises sensors, which can be either analog or digital, that will take input from the physical world using input sensors that are connected to the hardware of the physical computing system, as shown in the following diagram:

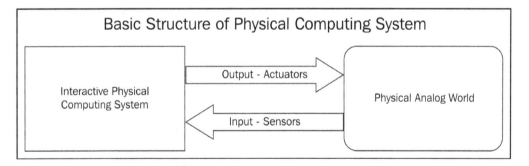

These inputs will be read by the software running on the electronic microprocessors and controllers on the physical computing system. Based on that software, a decision will be taken to provide the output and this output is converted from digital to analog form or makes a change in the physical world depending on the type of the actuators. So, basically, an action is being carried out based on the senses just like a human reflex actions and how they react to different senses. So the microcontroller or the computer chip that runs the software together acts as a brain and takes decisions based on the senses using the sensors connected to the hardware.

Let's look at a basic real-time example as discussed earlier to get a clear understanding of how the system works. A treadmill is a device people generally use for walking or running while staying in the same place, to do workouts in the gym, or some people even have them in their homes. These are powered by electric motors and have a sensor to read the speed at which the motor is running and a microcontroller unit / computer system with displays and buttons which runs a special software which reads these inputs from the sensor to measure speed as well as get input from the user to make the treadmill work at a particular speed. Shown in the following figure is a basic treadmill and below that you can see a basic block diagram as well:

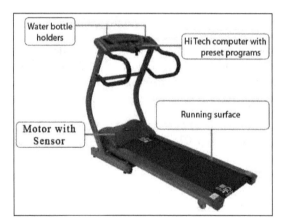

So, basically, as you see in the preceding figure, the treadmill has a HiTech computer console with buttons and a basic display for the user to select the speed at which he wants to run. The computer is connected to the motor controller to operate the motor at that particular speed by reading the speed sensor to measure the speed and regulate it using the algorithms running on the computer and the output from the computer controls to the motor controller maintain the speed of the motor. If you have a look at the following figure, you will understand better, as the block diagram shows the operation clearly:

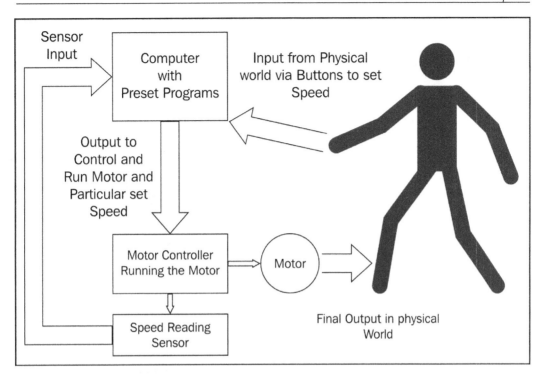

Looking at the treadmill example will have given you a clear idea about the basic structure of physical computing systems and their operation. Let's go ahead and look in detail at the electronics in the total hardware of the system, followed by how the software works with this hardware to make decisions and give input.

Before we discuss the hardware structure of physical computing systems, let's have a quick look at basic computer structure, as shown in the following diagram, as physical computing systems have evolved from computing systems basically; the structure of physical computing systems includes basic computing systems with added interfaces:

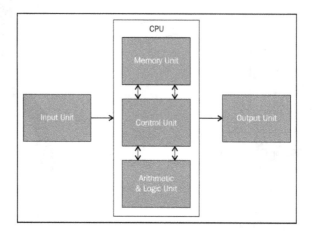

Shown above is the block diagram of a basic computer which contains the **central processing unit** (**CPU**) which stores data in the memory unit and processes it in the arithmetic and logic unit, and the control unit basically performs the data transfer between all the other units to make them work together. To the CPU we the Input and Output are interfaced. If you look at the following image of a basic computer, you can see that the system unit is the CPU, the monitor and speakers are output devices, and, similarly, the keyboard and mouse are input devices:

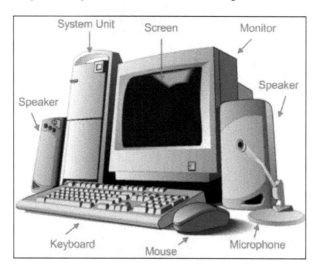

Based on the software running on the CPU, the input from keyboard and mouse carry out the process on the hardware and we can see the output in the monitor as well as hear via the speaker. The computers are advanced physical computing systems which have dedicated software, the operating systems running on them, and various protocols for communication. Now that we have clarity on how the computing system is structured, let's have a look at the structure of embedded hardware systems such as BeagleBone Black. We will look into the basic structure first, followed by a detailed hardware block diagram specific to BeagleBone Black:

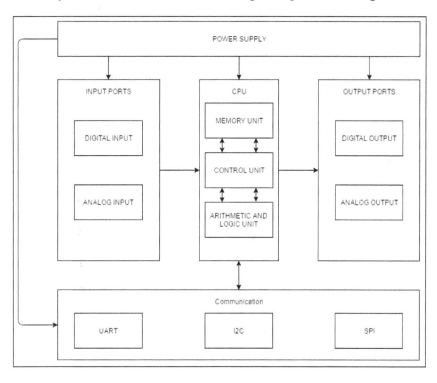

Shown in the preceding diagram is the fundamental block diagram of any physical computing embedded hardware system, in other words, embedded systems with microcontrollers and microprocessers. Comparing the preceding block diagram and the basic block diagram of the computer, you can see that the input and output ports are elaborated and explained well in the preceding block diagram, where you can see digital and analog input ports are interfaced with the CPU and, similarly, we have the output ports with Analog and Digital outputs. We also have the communication ports such as UART, I2C, SPI, and so on.

In basic terms, Digital input ports are capable of reading a particular DC voltage or a range of DC voltages between two set limits as HIGH and similarly as set limit as LOW value, in other words, the 1 and 0 we use in computer language called digital HIGH and digital LOW respectively. An example of a digital input can be the press of a switch: when it's closed, it's HIGH, in other words, 1, and when it's open, it's LOW, in other words, 0. Analog input ports are those which take in Analog voltage between a range of values and convert them to digital output form to make it understandable to the CPU by converting it to 0s and 1s or digital HIGHs and LOWs. An example of an Analog input could be an analog temperature sensor which senses temperature around it and provides a voltage in the range from minimum value to maximum value corresponding to the temperature around the sensor. Converters that convert Analog voltage values to digital values are called **Analog to Digital converters** (**ADCs**). Similarly, there are Digital output ports that provide HIGH and LOW values only and there are Analog output ports that convert digital values to Analog Outputs. An example of Analog output could be the audio output you get from phones and music players or video through an Analog signal. And we also have the communication ports, which include different protocol-based communication ports such as UART, I2C, SPI, and so on. The availability of input, output, and communication ports varies from one device to another, depending on what microcontrollers or microprocessors they use and the architecture of the system.

Now, let's look in detail at what the hardware structure of BeagleBone Black looks like, as shown in the following diagram:

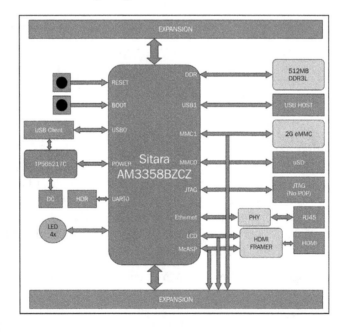

So, as you can see in the preceding block diagram, the CPU consists of a Sitara AM3358BZCZ processor, with 2 GB of eMMC storage as **Read Only Memory (ROM)** and 512 MB of **Random Access Memory (RAM)** with different external ports for interfaces such as HDMI for video, USB client for USB communication, RJ45 ports for Internet access, and so on. The structure is similar to a basic computer, just as we know that the BeagleBone board is nothing but a single board computer with GPIOs. The expansion header block contains the GPIOs, which can made to act as digital input or digital output depending on how we desire it to work for us based on the software running on the processor. The expansion headers also include analog inputs to read analog values. I believe that this section might have given you a clear idea about the basic structure of physical computing systems and how our BeagleBone board is also structured in a similar way.

Application areas

A few of the application areas where physical computing systems are used include almost all of modern-day technology gadgets and machines, from your mobile phones, fire alarms, and baby monitors, to home automation and industrial automation electronic systems, as well as the robotic systems used in homes and industries.

For example, what fire alarms with sprinkler systems in malls do is, basically, sense the temperature and smoke using sensors and whenever a event of fire is detected, they start the sprinkler system to sprinkle water from the tanks via the pipes and pumps using a control system that is continuously running the dedicated software that was written to do this operation.

Similarly, home automation systems, baby monitors that are connected to the Internet help you connect your home electronic devices to the Internet and dedicated artificial intelligence software programs running on the servers operate your air conditioning or lighting and heating, and so on, to make your life better. Similar applications are also seen in industry, where robots are making a huge difference in manufacturing industries and nowadays many robot bartender systems are in use.

So, I hope now you should be able to imagine a clear picture of the existence of physical computing systems around us and how they work.

In the sections and chapters coming after this, we will look into the building of different projects and use of these ports available on the expansion headers, including the digital inputs and outputs and Analog inputs to sense the input given from the physical world and build software by writing code on Python to make the system respond and act by providing output depending on the sensed input based on the software.

Project – toggle LED using a push button

Now that we have a clear idea about what physical computing systems are and how they work, let's go ahead and build our own physical computing system using BeagleBone Black by connecting a push button switch to act as a input to the system and an LED which will act as the output. How we write the software program will decide what the LED does based on the input from the push button switch.

We already know how to connect an LED to the BeagleBone board and also how to program in Python to turn on and turn off the LED just as we experimented in the project of the last chapter. In this project, we will use the knowledge we gained and what we are going to learn now before we go ahead and build the physical computing system. Now that we know how to interface an LED, let's learn how to interface a push button and read input value from the push button connected to the BeagleBone board using Python.

First, connect the push button to BeagleBone Black, as shown in the following figure:

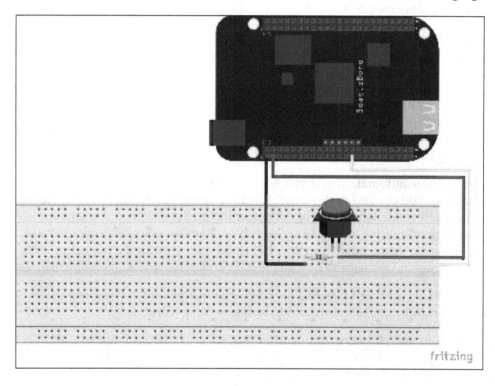

Once you have connected the push button switch to BeagleBone Black as shown in the preceding figure to the GPIO_115 / P9_27 pin on the GPIO header through the switch and resistor to pull down the state to LOW when the push button is not pressed, let's go ahead and read the input from the switch via the python interactive shell.

Pull-down and pull-up resistors are used to keep the input state with either low or high input supplied as input to the GPIO pin. You can do your own research on the Web to learn more about pull-down and pull-up resistors.

Open the Python interactive shell:

```
debian@beaglebone:~/WorkSpace$ sudo python
Python 2.7.3 (default, Mar 14 2014, 17:55:54)
[GCC 4.6.3] on linux2
Type "help", "copyright", "credits" or "license" for more information.
>>>
```

Import the GPIO library using the following line of code:

```
import Adafruit_BBIO.GPIO as GPIO
```

```
>>> import Adafruit_BBIO.GPIO as GPIO
>>>
```

Then let's define GPIO P9_27 of BeagleBone Black as the input pin to which we have connected the switch using the following command:

```
GPIO.setup("P9_27", GPIO.IN)
```

```
>>> import Adafruit_BBIO.GPIO as GPIO
>>> GPIO.setup("P9_27", GPIO.IN)
```

Next, read the current status of the GPIO using the following command:

```
GPIO.input("P9_27")
```

```
>>> import Adafruit_BBIO.GPIO as GPIO
>>> GPIO.setup("P9_27", GPIO.IN)
>>> GPIO.input("P9_27")
0
```

That should print out the current status of GPIO P9_27; in the output shown in the preceding screenshot, it is 0. Now the setup is as shown in the following image, where the button is not pressed; that is the reason the reading value of P9_27 GPIO is 0:

When you press the push button and hold it and then read the input, you will get the input value as 1, as shown in the following screenshot:

```
>>> GPIO.input("P9_27")
1
```

So, as shown in the preceding screenshot, when the button is pressed, the value that will be read is 1, as shown in the preceding screenshot on the python console:

Now that we know the basic functions using which we can read the input status of the push button, let's go ahead and write the python program which will read the push button status in real time and print it every half a second.

First, let's create the python file:

```
debian@beaglebone:~/WorkSpace$ sudo nano ButtonTest.py
```

Then, let us type the program as shown in the following screenshot and save it:

```
 debian@beaglebone: ~/WorkSpace                               —    □    ×

  GNU nano 2.2.6                    File: ButtonTest.py                    ^

import Adafruit_BBIO.GPIO as GPIO
import time
GPIO.setup("P9_27", GPIO.IN)
while True:
        print GPIO.input("P9_27")
        time.sleep(0.5)




^G Get Help   ^O WriteOut   ^R Read File ^Y Prev Page ^K Cut Text  ^C Cur Pos
^X Exit       ^J Justify    ^W Where Is  ^V Next Page ^U UnCut Text^T To Spell  v
```

Next we will run the Python code:

```
debian@beaglebone:~/WorkSpace$ sudo python ButtonTest.py
0
0
0
```

When you run the python code, the output will be as shown in the preceding screenshot when you don't press the push button.

And when you press and hold it, the output will be as shown in the following screenshot:

```
0
0
1
1
1
```

When you leave the button again and leave it to come back to its previous position, the output will be as shown in the following screenshot:

```
1
1
0
0
0
```

Now let's go ahead and modify the code in such a way that, instead of printing the current status of the switch, the python program prints that the button was pressed every time you press it and leave it. Save the python code with the name `ButtonPress.py`:

```
debian@beaglebone: ~/WorkSpace
  GNU nano 2.2.6              File: ButtonPress.py

import Adafruit_BBIO.GPIO as GPIO
import time

GPIO.setup("P9_27", GPIO.IN)

old_switch_state = 0

while True:
    new_switch_state = GPIO.input("P9_27")
    if new_switch_state == 1 and old_switch_state == 0 :
        print('Button pressed!')
        time.sleep(0.1)
    old_switch_state = new_switch_state


                                  [ Read 13 lines ]
^G Get Help   ^O WriteOut   ^R Read File  ^Y Prev Page  ^K Cut Text   ^C Cur Pos
^X Exit       ^J Justify    ^W Where Is   ^V Next Page  ^U UnCut Text ^T To Spell
```

When you run the code and press the button, you will get the output as shown in the following screenshot:

```
debian@beaglebone:~/WorkSpace$ sudo python ButtonPress.py
Button pressed!
```

Every time you press the push button switch and leave it, you will get the text **Button pressed!** printed on the shell.

Now that we have the basic logic figured out to print the button press event, we will go ahead and modify this code to toggle the LED to on and off every time the button is pressed.

Before we move on to programming BeagleBone Black to toggle the LED, let's connect the LED to BeagleBone Black, as shown in the following circuit diagram with the push button switch as well:

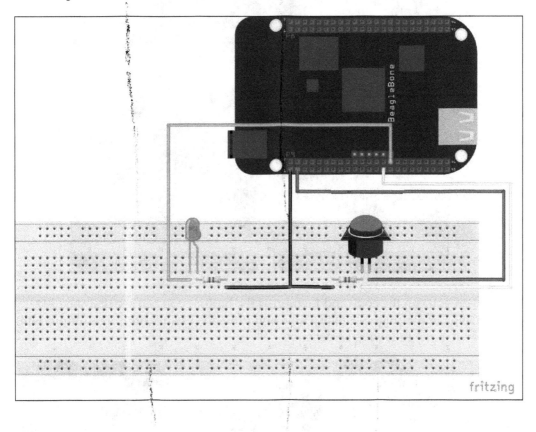

Now, write the program to toggle the LED to the On and Off state alternatively for every press of the button, as shown in the following screenshot, and save the file with the name `ButtonLEDToggle.py` or a name of your choice:

```
debian@beaglebone: ~/WorkSpace                                    —    □    ×
 GNU nano 2.2.6              File: ButtonLEDToggle.py                  Modified

import Adafruit_BBIO.GPIO as GPIO
import time

GPIO.setup("P9_27", GPIO.IN)
GPIO.setup("P9_30", GPIO.OUT)
GPIO.output("P9_30", GPIO.LOW)

old_switch_state = 0
ledstate = 0

while True:
    new_switch_state = GPIO.input("P9_27")
    if new_switch_state == 1 and old_switch_state == 0 :
        if ledstate == 0:
            GPIO.output("P9_30", GPIO.HIGH)
            print "Led On"
            ledstate = 1
        else:
            GPIO.output("P9_30", GPIO.LOW)
            print "Led Off"
            ledstate = 0
    time.sleep(0.1)
    old_switch_state = new_switch_state

File Name to Write: ButtonLEDToggle.py
^G Get Help      M-D DOS Format    M-A Append       M-B Backup File
^C Cancel        M-M Mac Format    M-P Prepend
```

Then, when you run the code and then press the button, you can see that the LED goes On and Off alternatively every time you press the push button. The output will be as shown in the following screenshot:

```
debian@beaglebone:~/WorkSpace$ sudo python ButtonLEDToggle.py
Led On
Led Off
Led On
Led Off
Led On
Led Off
Led On
```

When the LED is off as shown in the following image:

When you press the button and leave it, the LED will turn on, as shown in the following image:

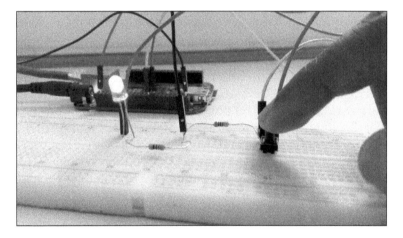

Again, when you press the button, the LED will toggle back to the Off state:

This will happen alternatively every time when you press the push button, the LED will toggle to HIGH and LOW state.

Summary

Here we are at the end of the chapter where we learnt the fundamental concept of how a physical computing system works with the help of the basic structure of these systems with BeagleBone Black as an example. We also discussed a few application areas in the real world. Then, we saw how to interface a push button switch with a BeagleBone board and write python code to read its status by accessing the GPIO pin as an input from python. At the end, we worked on a very basic project to understand how we can build our own physical computing system that senses and reacts to the physical world using a push button and LED to toggle the LED from On to Off every time you push the button.

In the next chapter, we will see how we can build a much more complex physical computing system with an Analog temperature sensor, unlike a digital input reading from the input from the push button we read. But before you go to the next chapter, I would suggest you write different programs to make the LED do whatever you like using the button press event; for example, you can count how many button presses have to be made and, based on that, you can make the LED blink for that many times and then get back to the mode where it will wait for the next number of clicks. Try anything that comes in your mind and play with the hardware and coding.

4

Real-time Physical Computing Systems Using BeagleBone

In this chapter we will be focusing on building a real-time physical computing system using BeagleBone board. We will be interfacing an LM35 temperature sensor module with BeagleBone Black in this chapter in order to understand how a sensor can be interfaced with BeagleBone board to make the system interact with the physical world. We will be getting ambient temperature as analog input readings from the physical world around the sensor, and coding the BeagleBone board to make the LEDs connected to the BeagleBone board to light it up in different colors, depending on the temperature levels measured by the sensor. So, by end of this chapter, you will have built an interactive physical computing system using BeagleBone board where it outputs LED indications based on the temperature measured. The contents of the chapter are divided into the following topics:

- Prerequisites
- Temperature sensor – LM35
- Interfacing the temperature sensor to BeagleBone board
- Simple project: Bicolor LED indicator that changes its color depending on the room temperature measured by temperature sensor

Prerequisites

This topic will cover what parts you need to get started with this chapter. These can be purchased from your favorite electrical hobby store, or can simply be ordered online.

Materials needed

- 1x BeagleBone Black
- 1x microSD card with the latest version of Debian flashed on it to boot the BeagleBone board from the microSD card
- 1x 5V DC, 2A power supply
- 1x Ethernet cable
- 1x LM35 temperature sensor
- 1x two-legged bicolor LED
- 1x 220 ohm resistor
- 1x BreadBoard
- A few male-to-male jumper wires
- 1x multi-meter (optional)

Temperature sensor

A temperature sensor is just an electronic chip that senses the ambient temperature around it and gives out varying voltage across the output terminal of the sensor. By using this, we can calculate the temperature that's being sensed. There are many different types of sensors available in the market, but we will be using the one that is the most easily available, and most commonly used by the hobbyist. This is the LM35 temperature sensor module, which is an analog output sensor, where the voltage can be directly converted to temperature values, based on the formula given by the manufacturer of the sensor, as mentioned in the datasheet of the sensor:

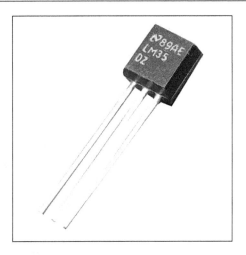

How do LM35 sensors work?

The basic principle behind the LM35 temperature sensor is that it converts the ambient temperature around the sensor to analog voltage proportionally.

In the following picture, you can see the pin terminals of the **LM35** temperature sensor where one terminal is the input, which gets supply input voltage, and the others are the output and the ground.

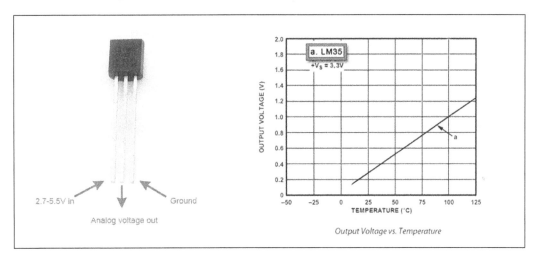

Output Voltage vs. Temperature

So, once you connect the power supply input to the temperature sensor with the ground, the analog voltage output that can be measured across the analog voltage out terminal, with respect to the ground, is as shown in the graph above.

For example, say the voltage measured across the output terminal and ground is 1 Volt, the ambient temperature in degrees Celsius is 100, which we can infer using the curve shown in the graph above.

And, from the datasheet of the LM35, we can infer that every 10mV is proportional to 1 degree Celsius. So we can use the formula given below to calculate the temperature in degree Celsius, if we know the analog output voltage in mV.

$$Temp\ in\ °C = (Vout\ in\ mV)°/10$$

To validate the temperature sensing and to test whether the sensor is working properly before moving on to the next topic of interfacing the sensor with BeagleBone board, you can use a multi-meter to measure the voltage across the output terminal while providing an external power supply to the LM35 temperature with common ground pin. Depending on the voltage measured, you can calculate the temperature using the previous formula. You can put hot or cold objects near to the sensor or hold them over it to see the voltage difference.

Temperature sensing using a LM35 sensor

Now that we know how an LM35 temperature sensor works, let's go ahead and look at the topic of measuring temperature with it by hooking it up to the BeagleBone board.

First of all, take three berg wires and connect the LM35 temperature sensor to the BeagleBone board, as per the circuit diagram shown in the following image:

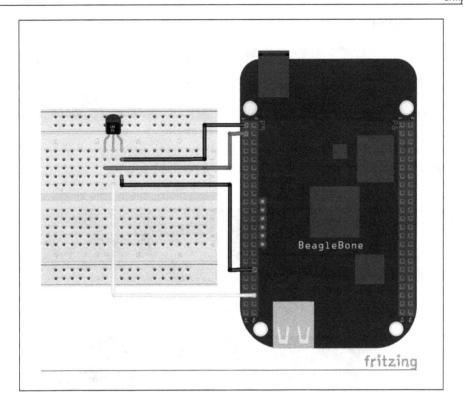

Then we will turn on the BeagleBone board, and then login into the Linux Shell to start coding it. We will access the WorkSpace folder where we are saving all the Python scripts that we've already created in the previous chapter. By now you should be familiar with how to navigate to the WorkSpace directory.

To do this, type command cd WorkSpace:

```
debian@beaglebone:~$ cd WorkSpace
debian@beaglebone:~/WorkSpace$
```

Once you are in the WorkSpace directory, and before writing the script to read temperature data, lets test it out via the Python console, which you should also be familiar with by now.

Type the command to start the Python interactive programming shell, `sudo python`:

```
debian@beaglebone:~/WorkSpace$ sudo python
Python 2.7.3 (default, Mar 14 2014, 17:55:54)
[GCC 4.6.3] on linux2
Type "help", "copyright", "credits" or "license" for more information.
>>>
```

Once we are inside the Python interactive shell, let us import the Adafruit GPIO library to read ADC inputs on the BeagleBone board, by typing `import Adafruit_BBIO.ADC as ADC`:

```
Python 2.7.3 (default, Mar 14 2014, 17:55:54)
[GCC 4.6.3] on linux2
Type "help", "copyright", "credits" or "license" for more information.
>>> import Adafruit_BBIO.ADC as ADC
>>>
```

Next we need to initialize the ADC, by typing the following command: `ADC.setup()`

```
>>> import Adafruit_BBIO.ADC as ADC
>>> ADC.setup()
>>>
```

To read the ADC reading on port `P9_40`, to which we have connected the output of the temperature sensor, use the following command:

```
ADC.read("P9_40")
```

The ADC ports available on the BeagleBone board are 12 bits, which equals $2^{12} = 4096$ units maximum, and the maximum voltage that can be given to these analog pins is 1.8 V. This means that the voltage input of these pins, varying from 0 to 1.8V, is proportional to 0 to 4096 ADC units, but in Python the Adafruit library gives us a reading between 0 to 1, which is proportional to 0 to 1.8V. The output of the ADC reading of the port `P9_40` using ADC read function is shown as follow:

```
>>> import Adafruit_BBIO.ADC as ADC
>>> ADC.setup()
>>> ADC.read("P9_40")
0.19555555284023285
>>> ADC.read("P9_40")
0.194444477558136
>>>
```

So you can see that the ADC reading on port `P9_40` is `0.19445`.

Now let's go ahead and save it on a variable to calculate how many volts it is. Let's create a variable `reading` and store the measured ADC reading as shown in the following screenshot:

```
>>> reading = ADC.read("P9_40")
>>> print reading
0.19555555284
```

Then, let's go ahead and convert the ADC reading into millivolts (mV). We know that the ADC is capable of reading 0 to 1.8V which is proportional to 0 to 1 unit of the ADC reading in Python, in other words 1.8 V = 1800 mV.

*Millivolts measured = (ADC Reading) * 1800*

*Voltage Measured = (ADC Reading) * 1.8*

That is to say, in our case, on the Python console you can create a variable named `millivolts` which will hold the voltage measured across the sensor output pin, with respect to the ground pin, as shown in the following screenshot:

```
>>> millivolts = reading * 1800
>>> print millivolts
351.999995112
```

As shown in the preceding screenshot, you will get the value of the voltage across the sensor output voltage pin in millivolts. Now, we can go ahead and convert the millivolts measured to temperature into degrees Celsius using the formula we obtained using the information from the datasheet at the beginning of this topic. This is shown in the following screenshot by creating a variable `temp_c` that holds the temperature in degrees Celsius:

```
>>> temp_c = (millivolts) / 10
>>> print temp_c
35.1999995112
```

```
>>> reading = ADC.read("P9_40")
>>> millivolts = reading * 1800
>>> temp_c = (millivolts) / 10
>>> print temp_c
35.1999995112
>>>
```

If we print the `temp_c` value we will get the output as shown in the preceding output.

Now, let's go ahead and write a Python program that will print the temperature sensor values every second.

Create the Python script file, `sudo nano TestLM35.py`:

```
debian@beaglebone:~/WorkSpace$ sudo nano TestLM35.py
```

Type in the code as shown in the following screenshot:

```
debian@beaglebone: ~/WorkSpace                                    —    □    ×
 GNU nano 2.2.6                  File: TestLM35.py                   Modified  ^
import Adafruit_BBIO.ADC as ADC
import time

ADC.setup()

while True:
    reading = ADC.read('P9_40')
    millivolts = reading * 1800
    temp_c = millivolts / 10
    print temp_c
    time.sleep(1)




^G Get Help   ^O WriteOut   ^R Read File  ^Y Prev Page  ^K Cut Text   ^C Cur Pos
^X Exit       ^J Justify    ^W Where Is   ^V Next Page  ^U UnCut Text ^T To Spell  v
```

Once you have typed in the code, you can go ahead and save it using the *Ctrl + X* command.

When you run the program you should see the output as shown in the following screenshot:

```
debian@beaglebone:~/WorkSpace$ sudo python TestLM35.py
35.1999995112
35.3000003099
35.3000003099
35.1999995112
```

So, in the preceding screenshot you can see that the ambient temperature around the sensor in degrees Celsius is printed every second. If you have come this far successfully, then you have successfully interfaced the LM35 temperature sensor with the BeagleBone board and Python. As a further step in this interfacing and testing of the LM35 with BeagleBone board, let's see whether or not the LM35 interfaced with the BeagleBone board is detecting any rise in the temperature by placing a lit matchstick near the sensor.

Place a lit matchstick near to the sensor as shown in the following picture:

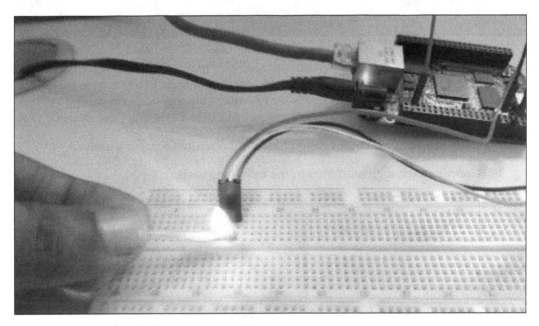

You can see that the temperature readings rise up when you bring the lit matchstick near to the temperature sensor, as shown in the following screenshot:

When you remove the matchstick from the sensor, it comes back down again as shown in the following screenshot:

```
68.8000023365
68.0000013113
66.9999986887
65.7000017166
64.1999977827
62.7999973297
61.700001955
60.6000012159
59.5000004768
58.6000013351
```

So, now that we know how to interface the LM35 temperature sensor with the BeagleBone board and read the temperature sensor readings, in the next topic of this chapter, which is our main project, let's build a real-time physical computing system using Python programming, by adding a bicolor LED to the BeagleBone board.

Intermediate project: LED color change based on measured temperature:

1. Connect the circuit as shown in the following picture:

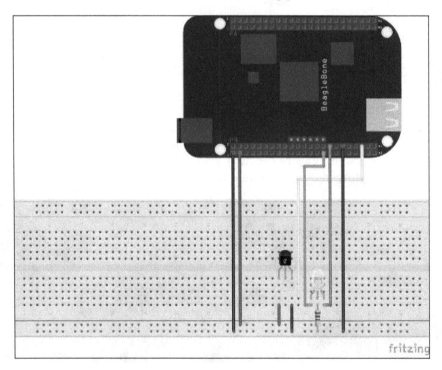

2. Write down the Python script.

As we already know how to interface a temperature sensor with the BeagleBone board and how to switch a GPIO on and off, to light an LED using Python, now we are going to combine both these previous experiments. Let's write a Python script to make the GPIO high or low based on the temperature value measured by the temperature sensor. Write down the code by changing the `TestLM35.py` file, as shown in the following screenshot, and save it with the different name `LM35nLED.py`:

```
GNU nano 2.2.6                    File: LM35nLED.py                    Modified

import Adafruit_BBIO.ADC as ADC
import Adafruit_BBIO.GPIO as GPIO
import time

RedLED = "P9_30"
GreenLED = "P9_27"
GPIO.setup(RedLED, GPIO.OUT)
GPIO.setup(GreenLED, GPIO.OUT)
GPIO.output(RedLED, GPIO.LOW)
GPIO.output(GreenLED, GPIO.LOW)

ADC.setup()

try:
        while True:
                reading = ADC.read('P9_40')
                millivolts = reading * 1800
                temp_c = millivolts / 10
                if(temp_c > 50):
                        print "Temperature is high"
                        GPIO.output(RedLED, GPIO.HIGH)
                        GPIO.output(GreenLED, GPIO.LOW)
                else:
                        print "Temperature is normal"
                        GPIO.output(RedLED, GPIO.LOW)
                        GPIO.output(GreenLED, GPIO.HIGH)
                time.sleep(1)

except KeyboardInterrupt:
    print "Keyboard Interrupt"
    GPIO.cleanup()
    print "GPIO Cleaned"

File Name to Write: LM35nLED.py
^G Get Help        M-D DOS Format     M-A Append         M-E Backup File
^C Cancel          M-M Mac Format     M-P Prepend
```

3. Now, when you run the code with the command, `sudo python LM35nLED.py` you should see the following:

```
debian@beaglebone:~/WorkSpace$ sudo python LM35nLED.py
```

Your setup should be like the one shown in the following screenshot in a room with an ambient temperature of less than 50 degrees Celsius:

The output for the Python program when you execute it will be as follows:

```
debian@beaglebone:~/WorkSpace$ sudo python LM35nLED.py
Temperature is normal
Temperature is normal
Temperature is normal
```

When you light a matchstick and hold it in front of the sensor, the output will be as follows:

```
Temperature is normal
Temperature is normal
Temperature is high
Temperature is high
Temperature is high
Temperature is high
Temperature is high
```

And the LED will go to red as shown in the following picture:

When you remove the matchstick from the sensor, it will change back to green.

```
Temperature is high
Temperature is high
Temperature is normal
Temperature is normal
Temperature is normal
Temperature is normal
Temperature is normal
Temperature is normal
Temperature is normal
```

Now we have a system that takes input (ambient temperature around the sensor) from the physical world, and based on that input changes something in the environment such as the LED color, with the information of the temperature getting printed out on the Linux shell. This brings us to the end of this chapter where we have built a basic physical computing system using BeagleBone Black.

Summary

In this chapter we have learnt about temperature sensors and how they can be interfaced with the BeagleBone board to obtain temperature measurements by connecting the sensor to analog input reading pins on the BeagleBone board. Then we wrote a code to make decisions based on the input obtained from the LM35 temperature sensor where the decision was to turn on a particular GPIO pin that is connected to a bicolor LED in order to change the color of the LED based on the ambient temperature around the sensor. So, in this way we have a real-time physical computing system up and running on BeagleBone Black using Python to get started. But this is just local computing where decisions are made based on the program running on the local system and all the data is in the local system itself.

Now in the next chapter, we will go ahead and build a more advanced real-time physical computing system, that is connected to the Internet, and on which the sensor data is sent to cloud server from the BeagleBone board that is connected to the Internet.

5
Connecting Physical Computing Systems to the Internet

In this chapter, we will be focusing on connecting the BeagleBone board to the Internet to connect the physical computing systems that we build to the Internet. First we will look into giving Internet access to the BeagleBone board via Ethernet, then we will learn how to add Wi-Fi capability to the BeagleBone board so that the system we build can be placed anywhere where we have Wi-Fi access, and so that we are not restricted to setting up the system only where the Ethernet is available. Once we are done with this, we will go ahead and build two projects; in the first one we will send an e-mail alert whenever the temperature sensor reading goes above a set level in the Python program running on the BeagleBone board. The next one will be a basic beginner project on Internet of Things for you to get started where the BeagleBone board will be uploading the temperature sensor data to a cloud server on the Internet. So basically, we will be using the knowledge we learnt in previous chapters, in this chapter, in order to take our previous projects to the next level. We'll do this by connecting them to the Internet and by performing operations on the cloud and on messaging services such as e-mail. The contents of the chapter are divided into the following topics:

- Prerequisites
- Giving Internet access to your BeagleBone board
- Adding Wi-Fi to your BeagleBone board
- Intermediate level project: E-mail alert fire alarm – the Python program will send an e-mail if the temperature sensor readings go above a set level

- Advanced project: Sensor data to cloud – a Python program will upload the temperature sensor data to an open source or freely available cloud service using the HTTP web service

Prerequisites

This topic will cover what parts you need to get started with this chapter. These can be purchased from your favorite electrical hobby store or can simply be ordered online.

Materials needed

Following are the materials that we will need before moving ahead:

- 1x BeagleBone Black
- 1x microSD card with latest version of Debian flashed on it to boot the BeagleBone board from the microSD card
- 1x 5V DC, 2A power supply
- 1x Ethernet cable
- 1x LM35 temperature sensor
- 1x compatible Wi-Fi dongle
- 1x BreadBoard
- A few jumper wires

Giving Internet access to your BeagleBone board

Giving Internet access to the BeagleBone board via the Ethernet is very simple. All you need to do is connect one end of Ethernet cable to the BeagleBone board, and the other end to a router with an Internet connection. The BeagleBone board will obtain the IP address dynamically from the router using DHCP and get Internet access. To check this you can just type in the following command:

```
ping www.google.com
```

You will get the response as shown in the following screenshot. This means you have a working Internet connection.

```
debian@beaglebone:~$ ping www.google.com
PING www.google.com (173.194.72.106) 56(84) bytes of data.
64 bytes from tf-in-f106.1e100.net (173.194.72.106): icmp_req=1 ttl=48 time=106 ms
64 bytes from tf-in-f106.1e100.net (173.194.72.106): icmp_req=2 ttl=48 time=104 ms
64 bytes from tf-in-f106.1e100.net (173.194.72.106): icmp_req=3 ttl=48 time=109 ms
```

Actually, what the ping command does is, it tests the connection and latency between two network connections. The ping command sends packets of data to the other network computer, in our case the `www.google.com` server, or the IP address of that server. You can see next to `www.google.com` in the output above, the global IP address of the server is shown. The picture shows how the ping command measures the time taken to get a response from that server computer, where the time is in milliseconds.

So, it's as simple as that to give Internet access to the BeagleBone board, running a working operating system such as Linux. This will automatically obtain the IP address from the Internet router to which it is connected using DHCP. But in most of the cases we will need a setup where the real-time embedded system is wireless which gives more flexibility in placing the system at any place for its operation instead of restricting the setup to be connected to Ethernet cable. The next topic of this chapter will focus on how to setup Wi-Fi access to BeagleBone board.

Adding Wi-Fi to the BeagleBone board

To add Wi-Fi capability to the BeagleBone board, let's connect a Wi-Fi dongle in the USB port available on the BeagleBone board, as shown in the following picture:

Once you have connected the USB Wi-Fi dongle you can check whether it is connected or not by typing the following command:

- `lsusb`: This is shown in the following screenshot where the USB Wi-Fi dongle is highlighted, that is **Atheros Communications, Inc. AR9271 802.11n**:

```
debian@beaglebone:~$ lsusb
Bus 001 Device 002: ID 0cf3:9271 Atheros Communications, Inc. AR9271 802.11n
Bus 001 Device 001: ID 1d6b:0002 Linux Foundation 2.0 root hub
Bus 002 Device 001: ID 1d6b:0002 Linux Foundation 2.0 root hub
debian@beaglebone:~$ iwconfig
lo        no wireless extensions.

eth0      no wireless extensions.

usb0      no wireless extensions.

wlan1     IEEE 802.11bgn  ESSID:off/any
          Mode:Managed  Access Point: Not-Associated   Tx-Power=20 dBm
          Retry  long limit:7   RTS thr:off   Fragment thr:off
          Power Management:off

debian@beaglebone:~$
```

Then type the following command:

- `iwconfig`: iwconfig will show you the details of the wireless LAN connection status, as shown in the previous screenshot, where you can see that wlan1, which is highlighted, shows the detail that is not associated with any access point as of now.

Our next step is to connect the Wi-Fi dongle to the Wi-Fi access point. To do this we will be using a program called `wicd-curses`, which is available in Debian by default.

To use the program we need to enter the following command:

- sudo wicd-curses

```
debian@beaglebone:~$ sudo wicd-curses
```

Once you execute the command you will get an interactive program window as shown in the following screenshot:

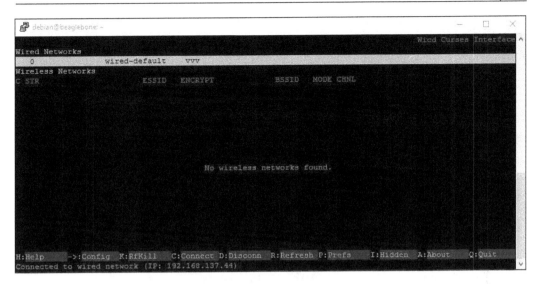

You can see in the preceding screenshot that the program states there are **No wireless networks found**. This is because we need to set up the USB Wi-Fi device first, and then search for the available Wi-Fi access points in the range. To do this, follow the next steps as shown in the following screenshot:

Press the *Tab* button once to open the configuration menu, – you should get the screen as shown in the following screenshot:

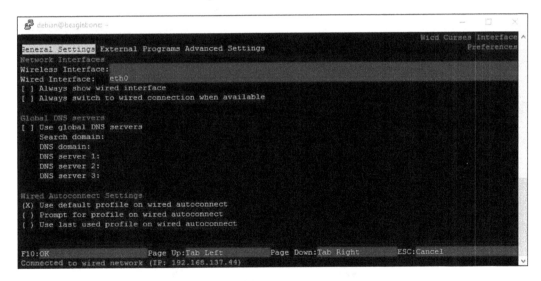

Once you get this screen, then press page up button once – it should highlight the wireless interface area, and then you need to type **wlan1** in it as shown in the following screenshot. If you remember, **wlan1** is what we had in the details of the wireless interface when we used the command `iwconfig` to get details of the interface created because of the USB Wi-Fi dongle.

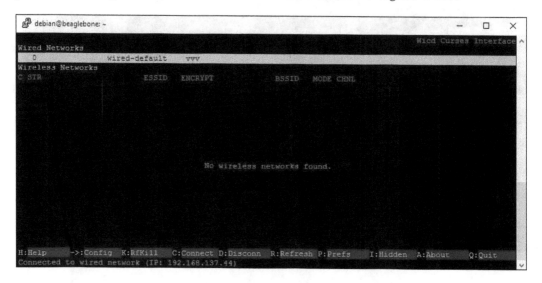

Then, press the *F10* key to save the configuration. Once you have saved it, it will take you back to the previous main screen as shown in the following screenshot:

Now you need to press the *R* key once to refresh the program and search for available Wi-Fi access points in the range that the Wi-Fi dongle can connect to. Once you press the *R* key you will get a screen as shown in the following screenshot saying that it's searching for available networks:

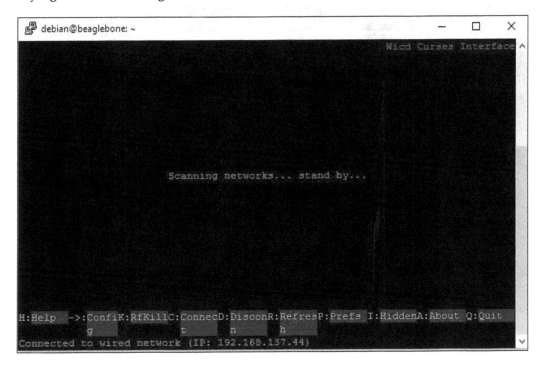

Then, after scanning, it will show the screen as shown in the following screenshot, listing out the available Wi-Fi access points in the range:

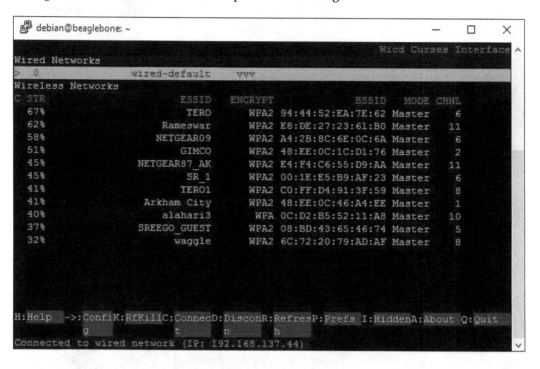

Once you have the list of available Wi-Fi access points you can choose the one to which you want the Wi-Fi dongle to connect by using the arrow keys up and down to select the access point. As you can see in the following screenshot, the access points get highlighted as you move the arrow keys. In this picture, **TERO** is highlighted:

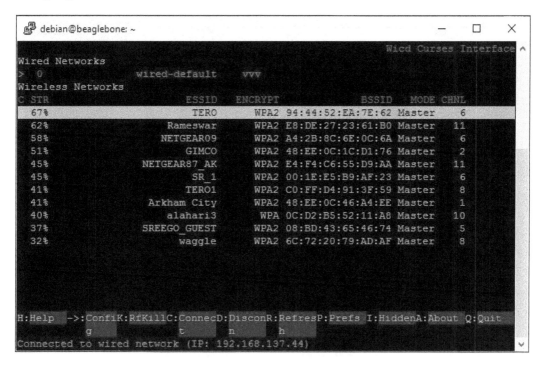

Once you have selected the network you want to connect to, when its highlighted as shown in the preceding picture, press the **right arrow** key on the keyboard and you should see the screen as shown in following screenshot which is asking for a password to connect:

```
debian@beaglebone: ~                                                    —   □   ×
                                                          Wicd Curses Interface ^
          Configuring preferences for wireless network "TERO" (94:44:52:EA:7E:62)
[ ] Use Static IPs
IP:
Netmask:
Gateway:

[ ] Use Static DNS                            [ ] Use global DNS servers
DNS domain:
Search domain:
DNS server 1:
DNS server 2:
DNS server 3:

[ ] Use DHCP Hostname
DHCP Hostname: beaglebone

[ ] Use these settings for all networks sharing this essid
[ ] Automatically connect to this network
[X] Use Encryption
WPA 1/2 (Hex [0-9/A-F])      vvv
Key:

F10:OK                                       ESC:Cancel
Connected to wired network (IP: 192.168.137.44)                                 v
```

You need to set the options as shown in the following screenshot to get a DHCP-based IP allocation from the router, or if you want to have a static IP for your BeagleBone board, you can do that as well. Use the *Tab* key to switch fields on the screen.

```
 debian@beaglebone: ~                                    —    □    X

                                                Wicd Curses Interface
        Configuring preferences for wireless network "TERO" (94:44:52:EA:7E:62)
[ ] Use Static IPs
IP:
Netmask:
Gateway:

[ ] Use Static DNS                      [ ] Use global DNS servers
DNS domain:
Search domain:
DNS server 1:
DNS server 2:
DNS server 3:

[X] Use DHCP Hostname
DHCP Hostname: beaglebone

[X] Use these settings for all networks sharing this essid
[X] Automatically connect to this network
[X] Use Encryption
WPA 1/2 (Hex [0-9/A-F])      vvv
Key: dailyship337

F10:OK                          ESC:Cancel
Connected to wired network (IP: 192.168.137.44)
```

So, set the hostname and enter the passkey in the key field as shown in the preceding screenshot, and save by pressing the *F10* key. Once you have done that you will get back to the main screen with a list of Wi-Fi access points available, as shown in the following screenshot:

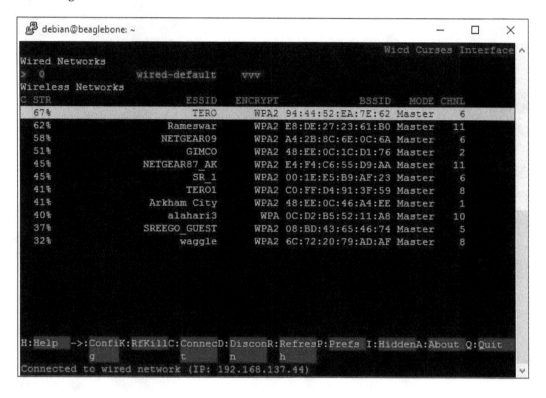

Now you can press the *C* key connect to the network. Once you press it, your shell connection will be lost, as the BeagleBone board will get disconnected from the network via the Ethernet connection through which you have logged in. Now, the BeagleBone board will connect to the network via Wi-Fi, so the IP address of the BeagleBone board must have changed. To check this, we need to login to the router configuration page of the same router as we used to connect to the Wi-Fi when we connected the BeagleBone board. Think back to what we did in the first chapter to find the IP address of the BeagleBone board connected via the Ethernet to the router. Now we need to do the same with the Wi-Fi connection.

Open the router page as follows:

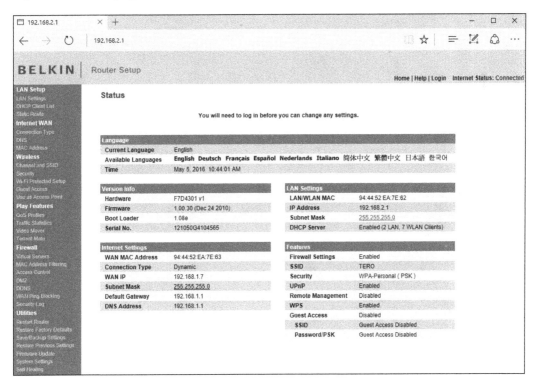

Check the list of DHCP clients:

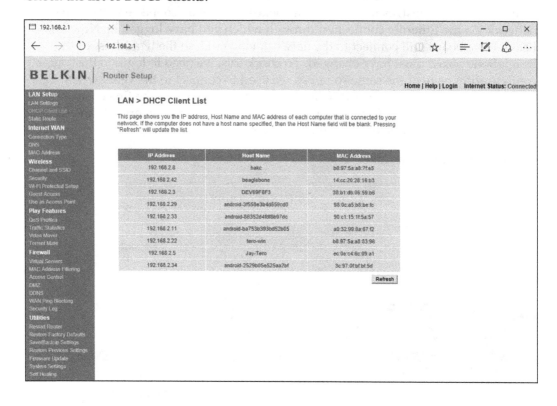

So, you can see the IP address of the BeagleBone board connected to the network via Wi-Fi and, if you remember, BeagleBone was the hostname we mentioned when configuring the Wi-Fi with our passkey. Now let's login into the Linux shell using this new IP address we have assigned:

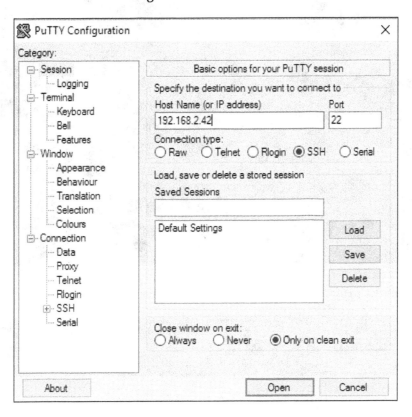

Once logged in using the same user ID and password, type the command `iwconfig` again, and you can see that wlan1 is connected to the SSID that we configured and connected, which you can see it in the following screenshot:

```
debian@beaglebone:~$ lsusb
Bus 001 Device 002: ID 0cf3:9271 Atheros Communications, Inc. AR9271 802.11n
Bus 001 Device 001: ID 1d6b:0002 Linux Foundation 2.0 root hub
Bus 002 Device 001: ID 1d6b:0002 Linux Foundation 2.0 root hub
debian@beaglebone:~$ iwconfig
lo          no wireless extensions.

eth0        no wireless extensions.

usb0        no wireless extensions.

wlan1       IEEE 802.11bgn  ESSID:"TERO"
            Mode:Managed  Frequency:2.437 GHz  Access Point: 94:44:52:EA:7E:62
            Bit Rate=135 Mb/s   Tx-Power=20 dBm
            Retry  long limit:7   RTS thr:off    Fragment thr:off
            Power Management:off
            Link Quality=50/70  Signal level=-60 dBm
            Rx invalid nwid:0  Rx invalid crypt:0  Rx invalid frag:0
            Tx excessive retries:0  Invalid misc:53   Missed beacon:0
```

Now type in the `ping` command to check the Internet connectivity:

```
debian@beaglebone:~$ ping www.google.com
PING www.google.com (173.194.72.106) 56(84) bytes of data.
64 bytes from tf-in-f106.1e100.net (173.194.72.106): icmp_req=1 ttl=48 time=106 ms
64 bytes from tf-in-f106.1e100.net (173.194.72.106): icmp_req=2 ttl=48 time=104 ms
64 bytes from tf-in-f106.1e100.net (173.194.72.106): icmp_req=3 ttl=48 time=109 ms
```

Once we have the Internet connection properly working on the BeagleBone board, we can move on to the next topics: two projects with the system connected to the Internet.

Intermediate level project: An e-mail alert fire alarm

First of all, as in the previous chapter, take three berg wires and connect the LM35 temperature sensor to the BeagleBone board, as per the circuit diagram shown in the following image:

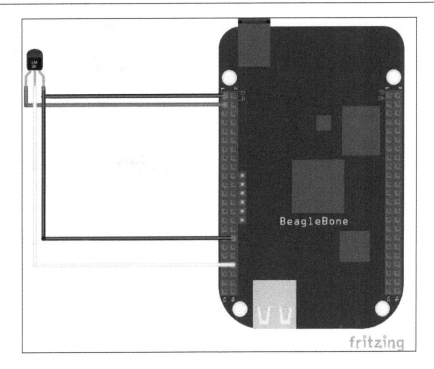

Then we will turn on the BeagleBone board and login to the Linux shell to start coding it.

Open the Python console to learn and test how to send an e-mail using Python:

```
debian@beaglebone:~/WorkSpace$ sudo python
Python 2.7.3 (default, Mar 14 2014, 17:55:54)
[GCC 4.6.3] on linux2
Type "help", "copyright", "credits" or "license" for more information.
>>>
```

Our first step will be to import the smtplib into Python, which is the mail transfer protocol library with the predefined function that we will be using in the program.

```
debian@beaglebone:~/WorkSpace$ sudo python
Python 2.7.3 (default, Mar 14 2014, 17:55:54)
[GCC 4.6.3] on linux2
Type "help", "copyright", "credits" or "license" for more information.
>>> import smtplib
>>>
```

Next create a variable to store the e-mail ID to which you need to send the e-mail:

```
>>> import smtplib
>>> to = 'letsplaywitharduino@gmail.com'
>>> []
```

Then create the variables where you need to store the e-mail ID and password of the account from which you want to send the e-mail:

```
>>> gmail_user = 'jayakarthigeyan@gmail.com'
>>> gmail_pwd = 'xzyxkxin@#$8'
>>>
```

Create an SMTP object with a Gmail hostname and port number **587**:

```
>>> smtpserver = smtplib.SMTP("smtp.gmail.com",587)
>>>
```

EHLO is just like HELO except that the server's response text provides computer-readable information about the server's abilities. The response of this helps us to confirm whether the SMTP server we created is at our service:

```
>>> smtpserver.ehlo()
(250, 'smtp.gmail.com at your service, [183.82.111.33]\nSIZE 35882577\n8BITMIME\nSTARTTLS\nENHANCEDSTATUSCODES\nPIPELINING\nCHUNKING\nSMTPUTF8')
>>>
```

Next we need to create a secure connection. We already have a connection, which we checked in the last step, but it is insecure. STARTTLS is a way to take an existing insecure connection and upgrade it to a secure connection using SSL/TLS. You can do this as shown in the following screenshot:

```
>>> smtpserver.starttls()
(220, '2.0.0 Ready to start TLS')
>>>
```

Once again use EHLO as shown in the picture below to check and create the running SMTP instance:

```
>>> smtpserver.ehlo
<bound method SMTP.ehlo of <smtplib.SMTP instance at 0xb6d4b328>>
>>>
```

Our next step is to create the header variable with information about the sender e-mail address, the receiver e-mail address, and details about the subject of the e-mail:

```
>>> header = 'To:' + to + '\n' + 'From: ' + gmail_user + '\n' + 'Subject:Python Email Test \n'
>>>
```

We need to create another variable where we will add the header to the message we are going to send in the e-mail.

When you print it out using the `print msg` command you can see how it appears in the following screenshot:

```
>>> msg = header + '\n This is test msg from BeagleBone \n\n'
>>> print msg
To:letsplaywithardуino@gmail.com
From: jayakarthigeyan@gmail.com
Subject:Python Email Test

 This is test msg from BeagleBone

>>>
```

Now we have the `msg` variable with information of the sender e-mail, receiver e-mail, subject of the e-mail and message of the e-mail as shown in preceding screenshot.

Our next step is to login to the server using the sender e-mail and password. You can do this as shown in the following screenshot:

```
>>> smtpserver.login(gmail_user, gmail_pwd)
(235, '2.7.0 Accepted')
>>>
```

If you get the response as shown in the preceding screenshot, then you have successfully logged in.

Next send the e-mail using the `sendmail` function with the receiver e-mail ID, sender e-mail ID and message as arguments:

```
>>> smtpserver.sendmail(gmail_user, to, msg)
{}
>>>
```

Once you have sent it you can go ahead and close the SMTP server and log out from it as shown following:

```
>>> smtpserver.close()
>>>
```

By now you must have received the e-mail on the receiver e-mail ID where you can see the subject **Python Email Test** just as we mentioned in Python, as shown in the following screenshot:

If you open the e-mail you can see this message:

We can actually see the message content is in a similar format to what we printed out on the Python console. Click on the **Show original** option on Gmail to see the original text e-mail, as shown in the following screenshot:

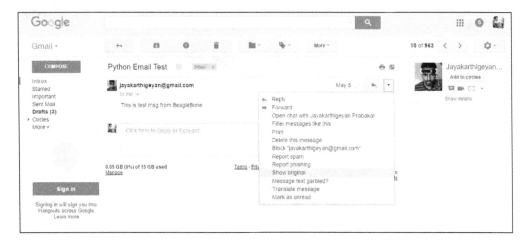

Once you click on **Show original** you will see the e-mail as shown in the following screenshot:

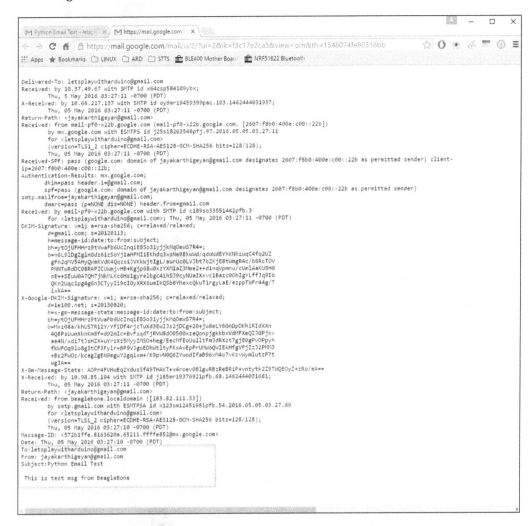

You can see the highlighted part in the mail, which is exactly the same as the message we composed and sent from the Python console, as shown following:

You can exit the Python console now:

```
>>> smtpserver.close()
>>>
KeyboardInterrupt
>>>
debian@beaglebone:~/WorkSpace$
```

Now let's go ahead and write the Python program to send an e-mail whenever the temperature goes too high. You can just edit the code from our project in the previous chapter and save it with a new name as shown in the following screenshot:

Once you have saved it, you can run the code as shown in the following screenshot:

```
debian@beaglebone:~/WorkSpace$ sudo python TemperatureEmailAlert.py
Temperature is normal
```

You should get an e-mail now as shown in the following screenshot:

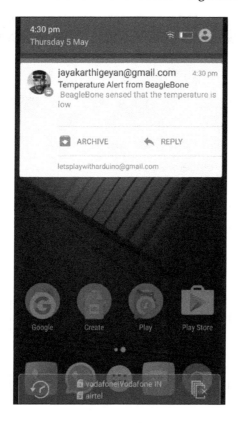

Hold a flame near to the sensor as shown in the following picture:

The output of the running Python code will be as shown in the following screenshot:

```
debian@beaglebone:~/WorkSpace$ sudo python TemperatureEmailAlert.py
Temperature is normal
Temperature is high
```

And you will get an e-mail as shown in the following screenshot:

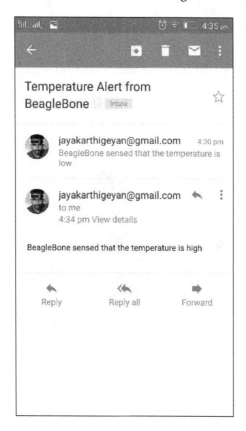

So, that ends our project. When you remove the flame, it will again send you an e-mail saying that the temperature is normal. Here is how the code works: whenever there is a change in the temperature level, that is if the temperature rises above a set or below a set limit, it will send an e-mail saying that the temperature is high or the temperature is low, respectively.

Unlike in this project, where a decision is made using the temperature measured with a temperature sensor, and then an email is sent based on this decision, the next project will directly upload the temperature sensor data to the cloud server.

Advanced level project: Uploading sensor data to a web cloud

The connections are similar to the previous project, the only difference in that will be writing a new Python program to upload data to a freely available cloud server using HTTP call methods.

With the same connections as the previous project, connect the temperature sensor to the BeagleBone board.

Then the first thing we need to do is setup the cloud server to which we need to upload data. We will be using a freely available cloud storage space website specially setup for IoT applications. The website is `www.thingspeak.com`, We chose to use this cloud solution out of the many available because ThingSpeak makes it very simple to upload data from hardware to a cloud for IoT applications. They have a lot of examples for different hardware development boards used for different applications. Looking at these wide variety of examples and easy APIs will help you experiment a lot more on your own using the BeagleBone board than what we do in this chapter.

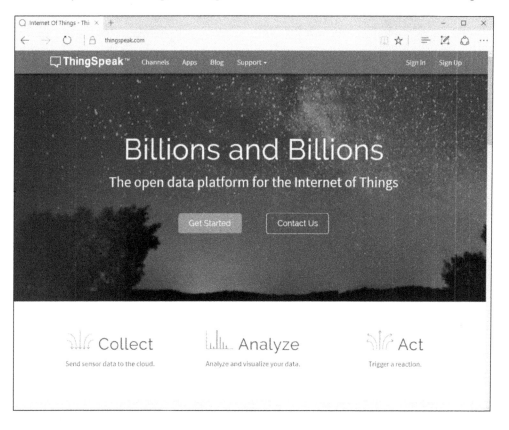

The first thing you need to do on this website is signup and create an account:

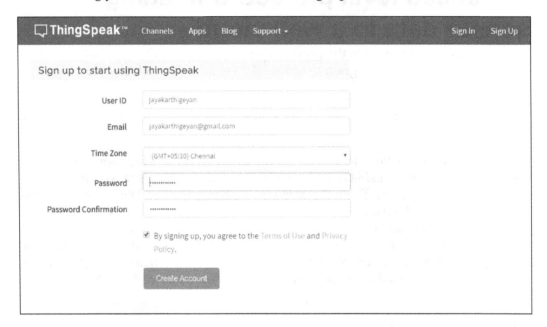

Once the account is created, and you can login into your account, you will see the screen as shown in the following screenshot, and will need to click on **New Channel**:

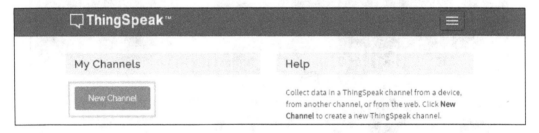

When you click on **New Channel** it will ask for details of the same. Fill them in as shown in the following screenshot:

Once you have entered the details you can click on **Save Channel**:

You can see the channel with the field as shown in the following screenshot:

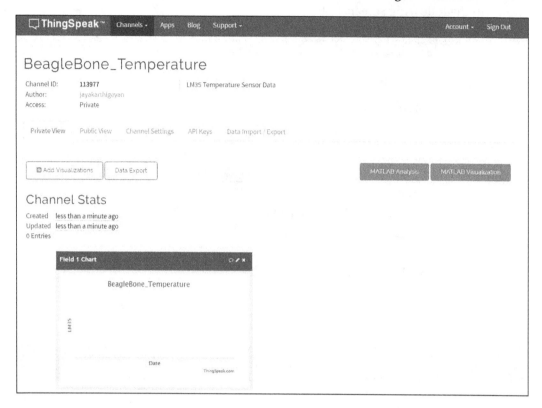

Next we should look at the API provided by the ThingSpeak website to update data to the cloud server.

You can see the details of the API of the HTTP call that you need to make to the ThingSpeak server in the following screenshot:

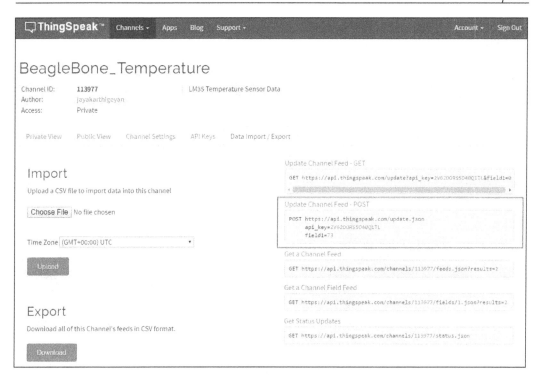

As highlighted in the preceding screenshot, we can use HTTP POST data to update data to the cloud server. The next steps will show you how to update data to the cloud server from Python using this HTTP POST call:

First, open the Python interactive console:

```
debian@beaglebone:~/WorkSpace$ sudo python
Python 2.7.3 (default, Mar 14 2014, 17:55:54)
[GCC 4.6.3] on linux2
Type "help", "copyright", "credits" or "license" for more information.
>>>
```

Then we need to import the `requests` module, which is a Python library that has built in functions to make HTTP requests on webservers:

```
>>> import requests
>>>
```

Next we can directly try making the HTTP POST request to the server using the API that was given as shown in the following screenshot:

The highlighted part is the parameter you pass to the server when you are make the POST call to `https://api.thingspeak.com/update.json` URL.

You can see that we have mentioned `field1=25` which will be updated on the ThingSpeak server.

The response will be stored in variable `r`, and when you `print r`, if you get the response as `200`, then the data was updated successfully:

```
>>> print r
<Response [200]>
>>>
```

Once you have the response as `200`, the data is updated on the webserver as you can see in the following screenshot:

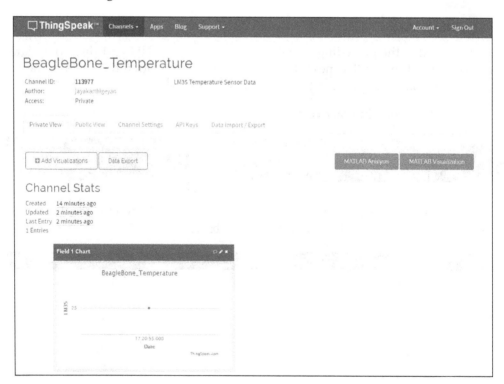

Perform the HTTP post call with `field1` data equal to `10`:

```
>>> r = requests.post('https://api.thingspeak.com/update.json', data = {'api_key':'2V62DORS5O40Q1TL','field1':'10'})
/usr/local/lib/python2.7/dist-packages/requests/packages/urllib3/util/ssl_.py:100: InsecurePlatformWarning: A true SSLContext object
is not available. This prevents urllib3 from configuring SSL appropriately and may cause certain SSL connections to fail. For more in
formation, see https://urllib3.readthedocs.org/en/latest/security.html#insecureplatformwarning.
  InsecurePlatformWarning
>>>
```

Then you can see that field1 is updated with new data at that time instant:

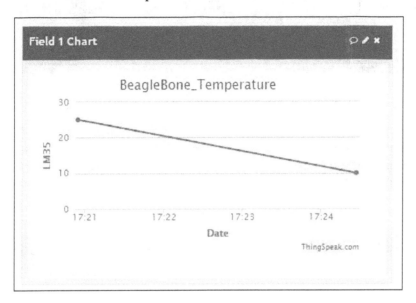

Now we will go ahead and write the code to update the temperature data to the cloud continuously. We can use our `TestLM35.py` code to make changes in it and save it with a new name to update the temperature data every 61 seconds to the `https://thingspeak.com/` server:

```
import Adafruit_BBIO.ADC as ADC
import time
import requests
ADC.setup()

while True:
    reading = ADC.read('P9_40')
    millivolts = reading * 1800
    temp_c = millivolts / 10
    print temp_c
    r = requests.post('https://api.thingspeak.com/update.json', data = {'api_key':'2V62DORS5O40Q1TL','field1':temp_c})
    if r == "<Response [200]>":
        print "Data Updated to Cloud"
    time.sleep(61)
```

When you run the program, the output will be as shown in the following screenshot:

```
debian@beaglebone:~/WorkSpace$ sudo python LM35ThingSpeak.py
33.4000012279
/usr/local/lib/python2.7/dist-packages/requests/packages/urllib3/util/ssl_.py:100: InsecurePlatformWarning: A true SSLConte
xt object is not available. This prevents urllib3 from configuring SSL appropriately and may cause certain SSL connections
to fail. For more information, see https://urllib3.readthedocs.org/en/latest/security.html#insecureplatformwarning.
  InsecurePlatformWarning
Data Updated to Cloud
33.3000004292
/usr/local/lib/python2.7/dist-packages/requests/packages/urllib3/util/ssl_.py:100: InsecurePlatformWarning: A true SSLConte
xt object is not available. This prevents urllib3 from configuring SSL appropriately and may cause certain SSL connections
to fail. For more information, see https://urllib3.readthedocs.org/en/latest/security.html#insecureplatformwarning.
  InsecurePlatformWarning
Data Updated to Cloud
^CTraceback (most recent call last):
  File "LM35ThingSpeak.py", line 17, in <module>
    time.sleep(61)
KeyboardInterrupt
debian@beaglebone:~/WorkSpace$ []
```

You can use *Ctrl + C* to end the program and exit.

Then, if you see the data on the field1 Chart on the ThingSpeak website, you can see that the data has been updated as shown in the pictures below. You can see the time stamp and see that the interval between the two instances of data update is 1 minute, and the temperature reading value also matches what we printed on the output on the console:

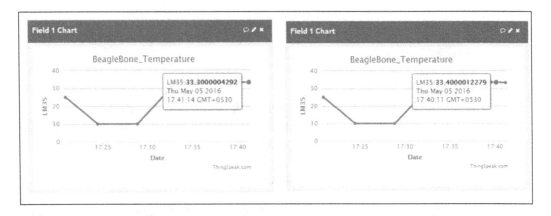

So, we have successfully written a program that updates data and stores it in a cloud server every one minute.

Summary

In this chapter we learnt about giving Internet access to the BeagleBone board through Wi-Fi, and sending an e-mail alert whenever temperature measured, using a temperature sensor connected to BeagleBone board, goes high or low, depending on the threshold value set in the program. We also saw how we can upload data to the cloud web server using HTTP requests made to the server from the BeagleBone board using Python. So, we have learnt how to set up basic level Internet of Things projects in this chapter. You can go ahead and explore the options of using the `requests` module in Python to use HTTP Put, Post, and Get requests on various freely available open source cloud servers built for IoT which are just like `https://thingspeak.com/`, which we used in this chapter. There are options where, instead of uploading data using an HTTP post request, you can get data from a cloud server; that is you can read data from the cloud server and print it on the Python program. You can read data from the server instead of uploading data, just like we did in this chapter. I would suggest you explore all such possibilities.

In our next chapter we will go ahead and set up our own web server and connect it to the Internet. Once you learn that, in future if you can have one BeagleBone board acting as a webserver, instead of the third-party server we used in this chapter, another BeagleBone board may be uploading data to the server we setup using another BeagleBone board.

6
Home Automation Using BeagleBone

In this chapter, we will be learning how to build a home automation system using BeagleBone Black. To get started, first we will be learning about Internet connected home automation systems and how they work. Then, we will move on to setting up Python Flask library that lets you run the HTTP server on your BeagleBone Black using Python.

Once we are up and running with the server using a Flask library on Python, we will use it to go ahead and create a program in which you can turn a GPIO on and turn off using the input from the webpage created by the server. This GPIO pin will be used to turn on and turn off an electrical relay to switch a lamp on and off.

The contents of the chapter are divided into the following:

- Prerequisites
- The structure of home automation systems
- An introduction to webservers
- An introduction to Flask for Python
- Setting up Flask for Python on a BeagleBone board
- Creating a webserver using Flask
- Transistors, relays, and power switches
- Advanced project: An Internet-controlled power switch – controlling an AC bulb from the Internet

Prerequisites

This topic will cover what parts you need in this Chapter. You can buy them from any electrical store or online.

Materials needed

- 1x BeagleBone Black
- 1x microSD card with latest version of Debian flashed on it to boot the BeagleBone board from a microSD card
- 1x 5V DC, 2A power supply
- 1x Ethernet cable
- 1x BreadBoard
- 1x relay board

The structure of home automation systems

This section will give you a basic idea about home automation systems that are connected to the Internet. In the following picture you can see that the mobile phone and the IoT devices are connected to Internet via the LAN Routers:

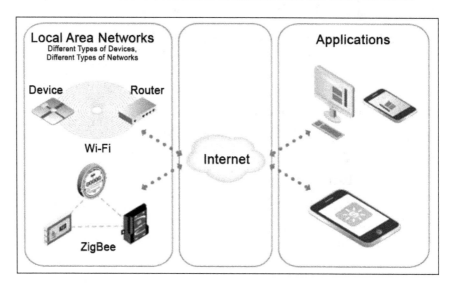

We will also be doing something similar in this chapter using the BeagleBone board, connected to Internet via our home router, to control an AC bulb using the relay circuit which is interfaced with the BeagleBone board. To do this, we will have setup a webserver on our BeagleBone board. We will see how to do this in the next topic of this chapter.

Introduction to web servers

Web servers are computers that are connected to the Internet, or intranet, to serve the requests that comes from the web browser of client computers or mobile devices. To understand this better, look at the following picture:

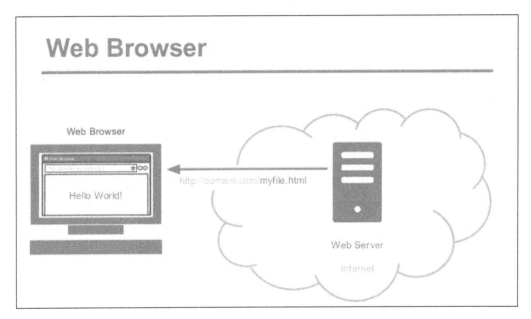

So, as shown in the preceding picture, a webserver is basically the computer which hosts the webpages and does the processing based on the requests sent from the web browser on the client's device. The client's device can be either a PC, laptop, mobile phone, tablet, or anything else which has a web browser, or a Linux shell that can make HTTP requests.

Go ahead and look at the following picture to understand this better:

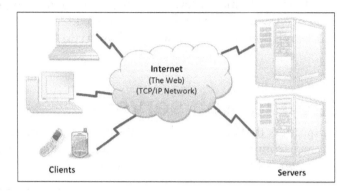

Now in this you can see that multiple clients are connected to multiple servers via the Internet, that is the **World Wide Web (WWW)**, **TCP/IP Network**.

What is TCP/IP? What exactly happens when you type a URL into your browser and hit enter?

Look at the following picture to understand more:

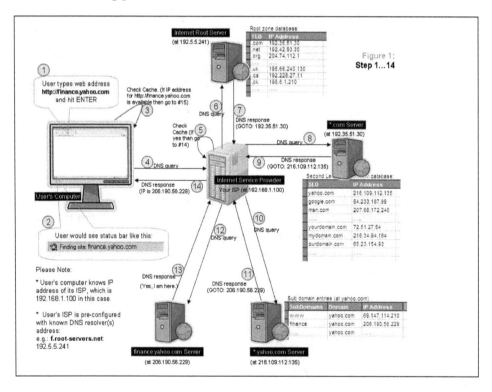

Similarly, in our system we have a webserver that goes through all the process as show in the preceding picture. A slight difference is that our webpage will be able to control the AC bulb. Now, that we know how webservers work, let's get ahead and setup a webserver on our BeagleBone board using Flask Python.

Python-Flask on BeagleBone Black

Flask is a Python framework to set up web servers using Python. In this topic, we will look at how we can set up a web server on BeagleBone Black using Python. The first thing we need to do to get started is to install the Python-Flask package on your BeagleBone Black from the Python package index. The steps below will walk you through how you can set up Flask and test it, followed by writing a Python code to interface it with your relay circuit. We will see this in the next topic followed by the main project of controlling an AC bulb from the Internet in the last topic of this chapter:

Step 1: Installing PIP as follows:

- `sudo apt-get install python-pip`:

  You should see that it's been already installed, since we have the latest version of Debian installed, and its already available in version. Some of the other versions might not have this, and it will be installed if it's not available, or upgraded if a newer version is available than the one that is installed in the current operating system.

```
debian@beaglebone:~$ sudo apt-get install python-pip
Reading package lists... Done
Building dependency tree
Reading state information... Done
python-pip is already the newest version.
0 upgraded, 0 newly installed, 0 to remove and 0 not upgraded.
debian@beaglebone:~$
```

  PIP installs and manages software packages that are written in Python. Many software packages can be found in the **Python Package Index** (**PyPI**).

Step 2: Install Flask-Python library as follows:

- `sudo pip install flask`

```
debian@beaglebone:~$ sudo pip install flask
```

Create a basic web application to test whether the package was installed successfully as follows:

Step 1: Create a directory on your BeagleBone Black:

- `mkdir HomeAutomation`

```
debian@beaglebone:~/WorkSpace$ mkdir HomeAutomation
```

Step 2: Change to the directory you created:

- `cd HomeAutomation`

```
debian@beaglebone:~/WorkSpace$ cd HomeAutomation
debian@beaglebone:~/WorkSpace/HomeAutomation$ []
```

Step 3: Create a Python file and write the code to setup a Hello World printing webpage server as follows:

- `nano WebApp.py`

```
debian@beaglebone:~/WorkSpace/HomeAutomation$ nano WebApp.py
```

Now type down the code on the file you created as shown in the following and save it:

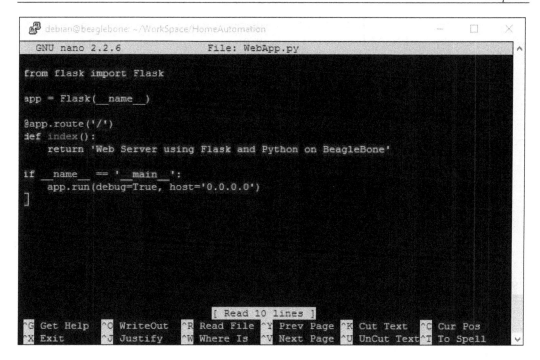

Step 4: Run the Python program as follows:

- ```
  sudo python WebApp.py
  ```

```
debian@beaglebone:~/WorkSpace/HomeAutomation$ sudo python WebApp.py
 * Running on http://0.0.0.0:5000/ (Press CTRL+C to quit)
 * Restarting with stat
 * Debugger is active!
 * Debugger pin code: 571-938-938
```

If you see the output as shown in the preceding picture, then you have done the previous steps correctly, and we have a server up and running on our BeagleBone board.
```

Now open the web server that we have running on the BeagleBone board by opening a webpage on the browser of a PC or mobile phone connected to the same LAN network to which the BeagleBone is connected. In order to do this type the following: `IPAddress_of_BeagleBone_Board:5000`, so, in my case, it would be `192.168.1.20:5000` on the URL address bar on the browser where `5000` is the default port number at which Python-Flask routes its connection. You can change this to different port numbers. Read more on the web to better understand different ports of web servers.

When you make the call to the server from the browser, you should see something like this:

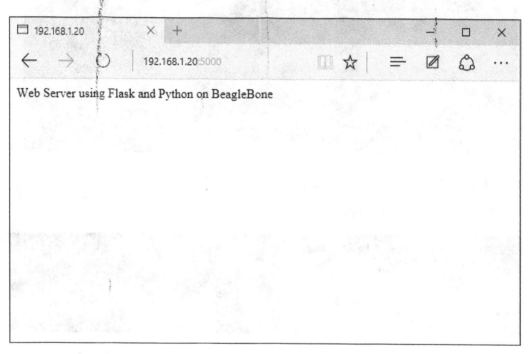

You will also be able to see the request call made by the browser to the server on BeagleBone as shown in the following screenshot:

```
debian@beaglebone:~/WorkSpace/HomeAutomation$ sudo python WebApp.py
 * Running on http://0.0.0.0:5000/ (Press CTRL+C to quit)
 * Restarting with stat
 * Debugger is active!
 * Debugger pin code: 571-938-938
192.168.1.4 - - [26/Jan/2016 05:43:33] "GET / HTTP/1.1" 200 -
```

Hit *Ctrl + C* to stop it:

```
debian@beaglebone:~/WorkSpace/HomeAutomation$ sudo python WebApp.py
 * Running on http://0.0.0.0:5000/ (Press CTRL+C to quit)
 * Restarting with stat
 * Debugger is active!
 * Debugger pin code: 571-938-938
192.168.1.4 - - [26/Jan/2016 05:43:33] "GET / HTTP/1.1" 200 -
^CException in thread Thread-1 (most likely raised during interpreter shutdown):
Traceback (most recent call last):
  File "/usr/lib/python2.7/threading.py", line 552, in __bootstrap_inner
  File "/usr/lib/python2.7/threading.py", line 505, in run
  File "/usr/local/lib/python2.7/dist-packages/werkzeug/serving.py", line 657, i
n inner
  File "/usr/local/lib/python2.7/dist-packages/werkzeug/serving.py", line 497, i
n serve_forever
  File "/usr/lib/python2.7/SocketServer.py", line 241, in serve_forever
  File "/usr/lib/python2.7/threading.py", line 389, in set
  File "/usr/lib/python2.7/threading.py", line 296, in notifyAll
<type 'exceptions.TypeError'>: 'NoneType' object is not callable
debian@beaglebone:~/WorkSpace/HomeAutomation$ 
```

Now that was a very basic thing we did using Python-Flask by echoing a text line.

Let's go ahead and do something using HTML layouts to make the web page look better. To do this create a directory called `templates` inside the home automation directory:

- `mkdir templates`

```
debian@beaglebone:~/WorkSpace/HomeAutomation$ mkdir templates
```

Switch to the new templates directory you created in order to create and save the HTML file inside it:

- `cd templates`

```
debian@beaglebone:~/WorkSpace/HomeAutomation$ cd templates
debian@beaglebone:~/WorkSpace/HomeAutomation/templates$ 
```

So this directory will be the place where you will find the HTML and CSS files through which you can route the web server to respond to requests from the client devices browser.

Now let's go ahead and create an HTML page inside this directory as shown in the following screenshot:

- `nano index.html`

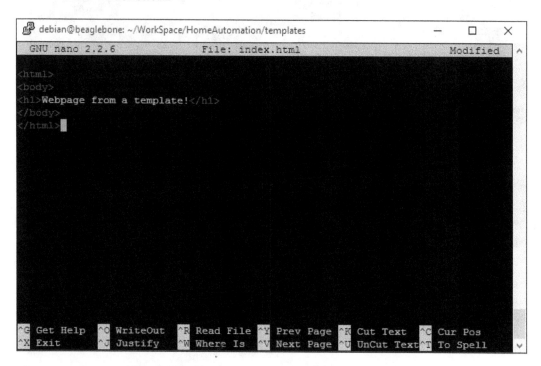

Once you are done with typing the content in the HTML file, as shown in the preceding picture, you can save the file by hitting *Ctrl + X* to save it. Once you have saved it, go ahead and switch back to the home automation directory:

- `cd ..`

```
debian@beaglebone:~/WorkSpace/HomeAutomation/templates$ cd ..
debian@beaglebone:~/WorkSpace/HomeAutomation$
```

Now we need to write a different program to route the web server to the HTML file that we created. Instead of writing something from scratch, let us modify the `WebApp.py` file that we created before and save it as `WebAppFromTemplate.py`, as most of the lines of code are same. See in the following screenshot:

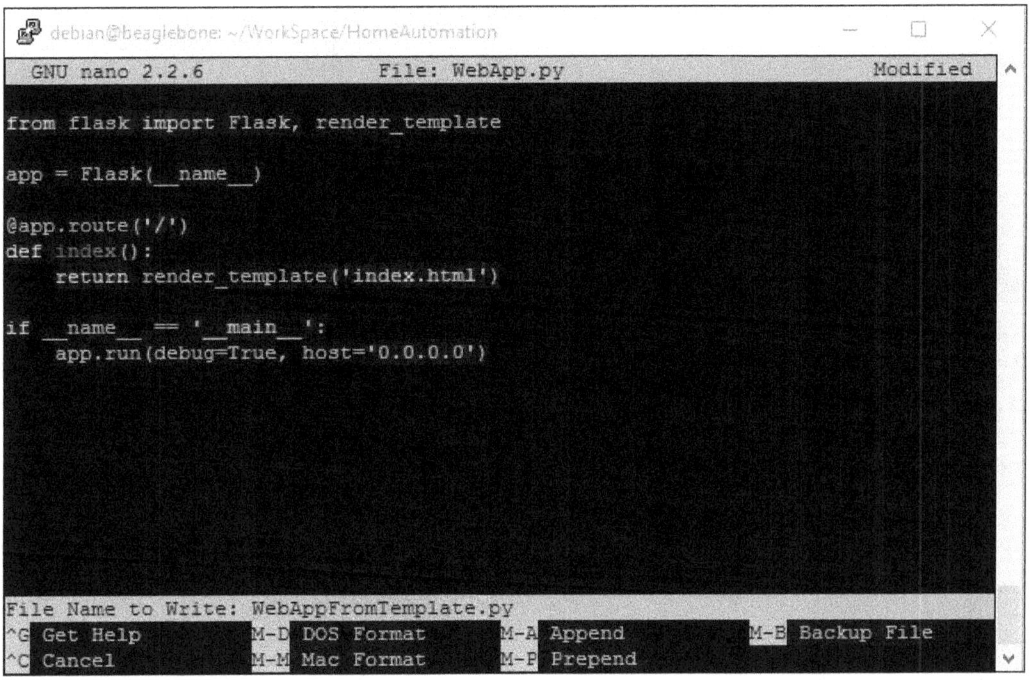

```
debian@beaglebone: ~/WorkSpace/HomeAutomation                    —    □    ×

  GNU nano 2.2.6              File: WebApp.py               Modified

from flask import Flask, render_template

app = Flask(__name__)

@app.route('/')
def index():
    return render_template('index.html')

if __name__ == '__main__':
    app.run(debug=True, host='0.0.0.0')



File Name to Write: WebAppFromTemplate.py
^G Get Help        M-D DOS Format      M-A Append        M-B Backup File
^C Cancel          M-M Mac Format      M-P Prepend
```

Once you have edited the file and saved it as `WebAppFromTemplate.py`, you can go ahead and run the code as follows:

- `sudo python WebAppFromTemplate.py`

Again, let's go ahead and open the URL from the browser and check the output. You should see something similar to the web page shown in the picture below:

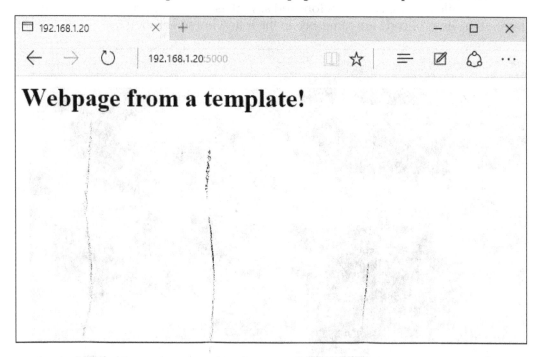

Now you can see that the text **Webpage from a template!** is formatted using HTML, and you can see it as an HTML based web page.

Like last time, you will see the HTTP call from the browser for debugging the shell:

```
debian@beaglebone:~/WorkSpace/HomeAutomation$ sudo python WebAppFromTemplate.py
 * Running on http://0.0.0.0:5000/ (Press CTRL+C to quit)
 * Restarting with stat
 * Debugger is active!
 * Debugger pin code: 571-938-938
192.168.1.4 - - [26/Jan/2016 06:04:40] "GET / HTTP/1.1" 200 -
```

For the project that we have in this chapter to control an AC bulb from Internet, we should have buttons on the web page instead of just the text that we displayed previously.

In order to have buttons on the HTML page we need to write HTML code for the webpage template and similarly we should write Python code to read the input when the buttons are clicked on the webpage. We can use these inputs to change the states of the GPIOs on the BeagleBone Black using Python code.

We will be looking into the details of how we can toggle the GPIO states from HTML button click inputs in the project section of this chapter. Before that, as the last part of this topic, let's create an HTML page with button inputs, read those inputs when they are made, and print a text that this particular button was clicked. We will have two buttons on the web page and these will be **ON** and **OFF**. Whenever any of these are clicked on the web page, the Python code will print that the particular button was clicked. Let's go ahead and do that.

First, switch back to the templates folder and create a file named main.html file with the content as shown in the following screenshot:

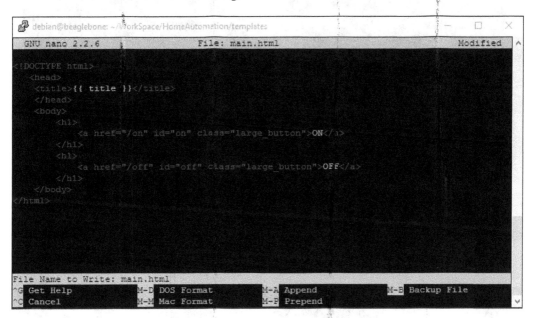

Now you can see that it has two button elements with ID on and off.

Once you are done with creating this file, save it and go back to the home automation directory, edit the file WebAppFromTemplate.py as shown in following screenshot, and save it as ControlWebApp.py:

```
debian@beaglebone: ~/WorkSpace/HomeAutomation                          —    □    ×
  GNU nano 2.2.6                   File: ControlWebApp.py                       ^

import time
from itertools import cycle
from flask import Flask, render_template

app = Flask(__name__)

@app.route("/")
@app.route("/<state>")
def update_lamp(state=None):
    if state == 'on':
        print "Button 'On' was clicked"
        time.sleep(.2)
    if state == 'off':
        print "Button 'Off' was clicked"                                       $
        time.sleep(.2)
    template_data = {
        'title' : state,
    }
    return render_template('main.html', **template_data)

if __name__ == "__main__":
    app.run(debug=True, host='0.0.0.0')



^G Get Help    ^O WriteOut    ^R Read File    ^Y Prev Page    ^K Cut Text    ^C Cur Pos
^X Exit        ^J Justify     ^W Where Is     ^V Next Page    ^U UnCut Text  ^T To Spell
```

Once you have saved it, you can go ahead and run the program as follows:

- sudo python ControlWebApp.py

```
debian@beaglebone:~/WorkSpace/HomeAutomation$ sudo python ControlWebApp.py
 * Running on http://0.0.0.0:5000/ (Press CTRL+C to quit)
 * Restarting with stat
 * Debugger is active!
 * Debugger pin code: 571-938-938
192.168.1.4 - - [26/Jan/2016 12:33:11] "GET / HTTP/1.1" 200 -
```

Now you can open the webpage and see how it looks. You should see something similar to the following screenshot:

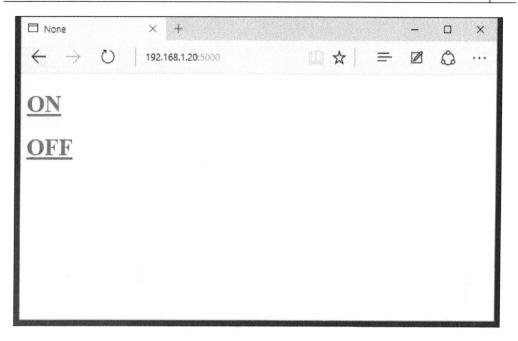

When you click on the **ON** button, you should see something like the following screenshot:

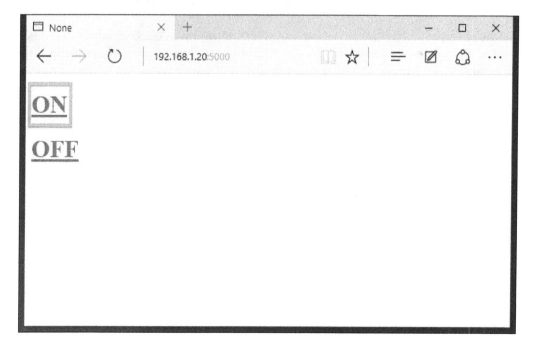

The output is as follows:

```
debian@beaglebone:~/WorkSpace/HomeAutomation$ sudo python ControlWebApp.py
 * Running on http://0.0.0.0:5000/ (Press CTRL+C to quit)
 * Restarting with stat
 * Debugger is active!
 * Debugger pin code: 571-938-938
192.168.1.4 - - [26/Jan/2016 12:33:11] "GET / HTTP/1.1" 200 -
Button 'On' was clicked
192.168.1.4 - - [26/Jan/2016 12:36:42] "GET /on HTTP/1.1" 200 -
```

When you click on the **OFF** button, you should see something like the following screenshot:

```
debian@beaglebone:~/WorkSpace/HomeAutomation$ sudo python ControlWebApp.py
 * Running on http://0.0.0.0:5000/ (Press CTRL+C to quit)
 * Restarting with stat
 * Debugger is active!
 * Debugger pin code: 571-938-938
192.168.1.4 - - [26/Jan/2016 12:33:11] "GET / HTTP/1.1" 200 -
Button 'On' was clicked
192.168.1.4 - - [26/Jan/2016 12:36:42] "GET /on HTTP/1.1" 200 -
Button 'Off' was clicked
192.168.1.4 - - [26/Jan/2016 12:37:45] "GET /off HTTP/1.1" 200 -
```

So now we have a program that can print which button was clicked. All we need is to write a program to change the state of the GPIO available on BeagleBone Black to HIGH and LOW whenever a button is pressed on the web page. We will be doing this in the project topic of this chapter. Before doing that, in the topic of this chapter, we will learn how a relay circuit works and how we can switch a relay circuit using the very little voltage that we get from the GPIO pins of the BeagleBone Black. In this way we will be able to use the relay to switch the AC Bulb on and off.

Transistors, relays, power switches

So basically, to switch an AC appliance or any circuit, you will need a switch, just like you have in your houses, where you have a switch to turn on a bulb or a fan. There is a basic circuit involved which looks very much like the following picture:

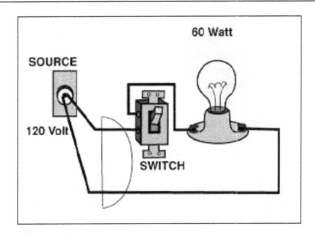

So, as we can see in the preceding picture, if you toggle the switch it's going to open and close the circuit. This in turn will make the bulb go off and on. But this is done mechanically in normal mechanical switches.

Whenever we want the same action to be performed, we will be using the electrically controlled switches, which are on an electrical relay. The image below shows an electrically controlled relay in off and on states:

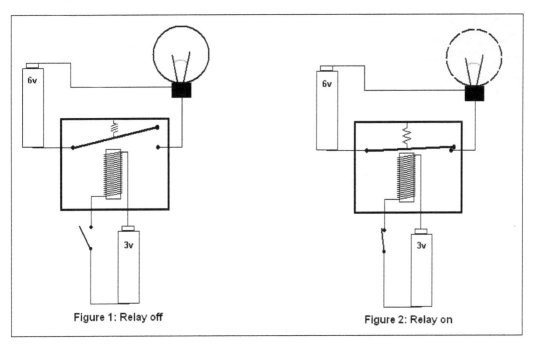

Figure 1: Relay off   Figure 2: Relay on

In the preceding diagram you can see that whenever the power is supplied to the coil from the **3V** power supply, the coil energizes and acts like a magnet pulling the terminal down. This connects the other terminal and closes the circuit and current flows through the circuit from the **6V** battery to the DC lamp. You can see this in action in Figure 2 in the preceding image. And when the coil is de-energized, as shown in Figure 1, the terminal is left open, which cuts off the circuit and opens it up so the lamp is in the off state, as no current flows through the circuit. Again, in the preceding example, you can see that a mechanical switch is used to switch the low voltage supply (3V) and the electrical relay is switching the high voltage supply.

Usually the easily available relays are off 5V DC operated where the voltage needed to energize the coil is 5V and enough current supply. But the GPIOs available on BeagleBone board are 3.3V at HIGH and 0V at LOW states respectively. We will be using a new electronic element in between to switch the low voltage supply, and this element is the transistor. I won't be going into details of types of transistor and their operation. You can browse around to learn more about it in detail. But in basic terms, it's an electronically controlled switch whenever base of the transistor is given supply i.e. on conduction happens via collector emitter and when base of transistor is low i.e. off, no conduction takes place.

Look at the following diagram to understand how our circuit is going to be with a transistor interfaced with the relay when the relay is used to make a connection for the AC Bulb:

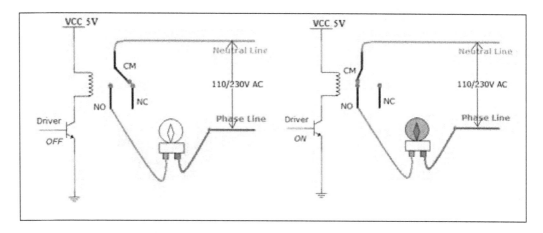

So whenever the base driver is ON, that is to say HIGH, it will switch on the relay and whenever the base of the transistor is OFF, or LOW it will switch off the relay and, in turn, switch off the AC bulb.

You can directory connect the base of the transistor to the GPIO of the BeagleBone board which will turn the transistor on and off whenever the GPIO pin is HIGH and LOW respectively.

Relays board are available that are ready-made with transistors and relays. You can directly interface these with BeagleBone boards or with any other microcontroller boards as you can see in the following picture:

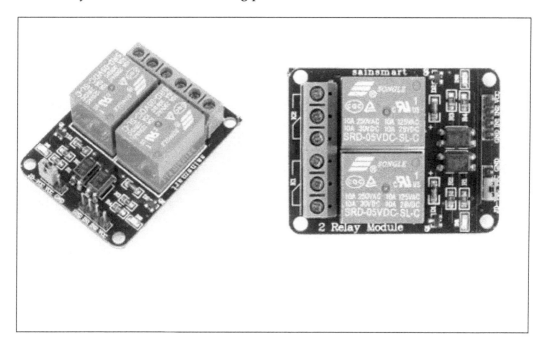

Getting one of these will make your work simple, but if you want to make one by yourself you can also do that researching it on the Internet. To make it easier for the next steps, I got one of the ready-made modules and interfaced it to the GPIO of the BeagleBone Black. The connections are pretty straightforward, as shown in the previous figures. D1 of the relay module is connected to GPIO_60 i.e. P9_12 and Vcc to 5V on BeagleBone Black, and the Gnd pin of the relay module is connected to the Gnd Pin of the relay module. Connect the phase and neutral wire from the AC bulb via the K1 NO and C terminals of the relay, as the D1 input corresponds to switching the K1 relay in the module.

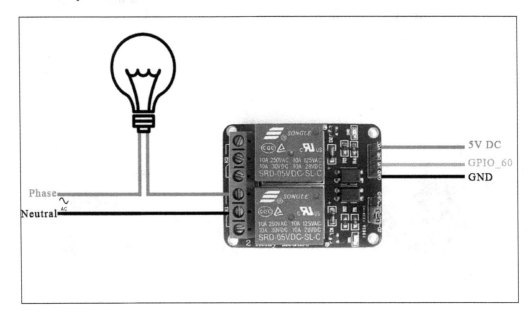

You can see the schematic given above for more clear details about the circuit connections.

Once you are done with the circuit connections, use the blink code that we used in the second chapter to test whether the relay is switching on and off, or else go ahead to the next topic to write down the code to control the circuit from the web page.

Advanced project: An Internet controlled power switch – controlling an AC bulb from the Internet

Now we have set up the circuit from the previous topic, we will code it on Python to switch the GPIO to HIGH and LOW from the web page. You can proceed and write the code as shown in the following screenshot:

```
GNU nano 2.2.6                    File: ControlWebApp.py                    Modified

import time
from itertools import cycle
from flask import Flask, render_template

import Adafruit_BBIO.GPIO as GPIO
GPIO.setup("P9_12", GPIO.OUT)

app = Flask(__name__)

@app.route("/")
@app.route("/<state>")
def update_lamp(state=None):
    if state == 'on':
        print "Bulb was turned on"
        GPIO.output("P9_12", GPIO.HIGH)
        time.sleep(.2)
    if state == 'off':
        print "Bulb was turned off"
        GPIO.output("P9_12", GPIO.LOW)
        time.sleep(.2)
    template_data = {
        'title' : state,
    }
    return render_template('main.html', **template_data)

if __name__ == "__main__":
    app.run(debug=True, host='0.0.0.0')


File Name to Write: GPIOControlWebApp.py
^G Get Help          M-D DOS Format        M-A Append        M-B Backup File
^C Cancel            M-M Mac Format        M-P Prepend
```

Now save the file as GPIOControlWebApp.py.

Let's run the code to switch the lamp on and off, and go ahead and open the page from the Android tablet. The tablet is connected to the same LAN Wi-Fi router as the BeagleBone board. Click the on and off buttons and you will see the output in the shell terminal as shown in the following screenshot:

```
debian@beaglebone:~/WorkSpace/HomeAutomation$ sudo python GPIOControlWebApp.py
 * Running on http://0.0.0.0:5000/ (Press CTRL+C to quit)
 * Restarting with stat
 * Debugger is active!
 * Debugger pin code: 571-938-938
192.168.1.14 - - [26/Jan/2016 14:02:45] "GET / HTTP/1.1" 200 -
192.168.1.4 - - [26/Jan/2016 14:02:45] "GET / HTTP/1.1" 200 -
192.168.1.4 - - [26/Jan/2016 14:02:45] "GET /favicon.ico HTTP/1.1" 200 -
192.168.1.14 - - [26/Jan/2016 14:03:05] "GET /favicon.ico HTTP/1.1" 200 -
Bulb was turned on
192.168.1.14 - - [26/Jan/2016 14:03:22] "GET /on HTTP/1.1" 200 -
192.168.1.14 - - [26/Jan/2016 14:03:22] "GET /favicon.ico HTTP/1.1" 200 -
Bulb was turned off
192.168.1.14 - - [26/Jan/2016 14:03:25] "GET /off HTTP/1.1" 200 -
192.168.1.14 - - [26/Jan/2016 14:03:25] "GET /favicon.ico HTTP/1.1" 200 -
Bulb was turned on
192.168.1.14 - - [26/Jan/2016 14:03:32] "GET /on HTTP/1.1" 200 -
192.168.1.14 - - [26/Jan/2016 14:03:32] "GET /favicon.ico HTTP/1.1" 200 -
Bulb was turned off
192.168.1.14 - - [26/Jan/2016 14:03:35] "GET /off HTTP/1.1" 200 -
192.168.1.14 - - [26/Jan/2016 14:03:35] "GET /favicon.ico HTTP/1.1" 200 -
Bulb was turned on
192.168.1.14 - - [26/Jan/2016 14:03:40] "GET /on HTTP/1.1" 200 -
192.168.1.14 - - [26/Jan/2016 14:03:40] "GET /favicon.ico HTTP/1.1" 200 -
Bulb was turned off
192.168.1.14 - - [26/Jan/2016 14:03:45] "GET /off HTTP/1.1" 200 -
192.168.1.14 - - [26/Jan/2016 14:03:45] "GET /favicon.ico HTTP/1.1" 200 -
Bulb was turned on
192.168.1.14 - - [26/Jan/2016 14:04:37] "GET /on HTTP/1.1" 200 -
192.168.1.14 - - [26/Jan/2016 14:04:37] "GET /favicon.ico HTTP/1.1" 200 -
Bulb was turned off
192.168.1.14 - - [26/Jan/2016 14:04:40] "GET /off HTTP/1.1" 200 -
192.168.1.14 - - [26/Jan/2016 14:04:40] "GET /favicon.ico HTTP/1.1" 200 -
```

And the bulb will turn on and off as shown in the following pictures:

Bulb is in the off state

Bulb is in the on state

But right now, we are just doing this on our local network within our home router LAN network to which the BeagleBone board is connected. What if we wanted to control the bulb via a 3G connection available on our phone? In this case you need to route your BeagleBone Black and connect to it via the Internet from your phone, which is connected to the Internet via 3G. If you go back to web servers topic in this chapter you can see that there are lots of routers, DNS gateways in between to connect to a server from one end of the Internet from a client to the server. In our case, our BeagleBone board device itself is acting as a server. We will be just be port forwarding our router to redirect the requests that comes to the router's public IP address to the particular port at which BeagleBone Black is hosting its server, that is 5000, in our case, the default port at which Python-Flask routes its requests. So, let's go ahead and do the port forwarding to access the web server on the BeagleBone board via the public IP assigned to our router by the Internet service provider.

Setting up port forwarding

Follow the steps to set up port forwarding:

1. As we did in *Chapter 1, Getting Started with BeagleBone*, login into your router's configuration page:

2. Go to **ADVANCED** settings:

3. Go to **Advanced Setup**:

4. Click on **Port Forwarding**:

5. Click on **Add Custom Service**.You will see the page as shown in the following screenshot:

Fill in the details and save the configuration by clicking on **Apply**:

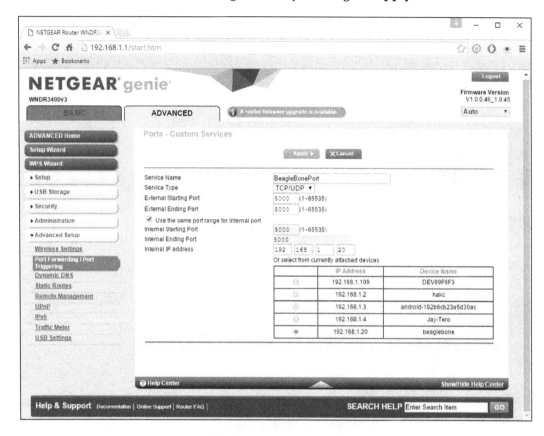

Once you are done with this. Go to Google and type in `what is my ip?` This will check your public IP Address, and you should get the output as shown in the following screenshot:

Once you have this, pull out your phone and connect to 3G, using this public IP address followed by port number 5000 to access your BeagleBone board. This will allow you to switch the AC bulb on and off from your phone. You will get a web page as shown in the following screenshot:

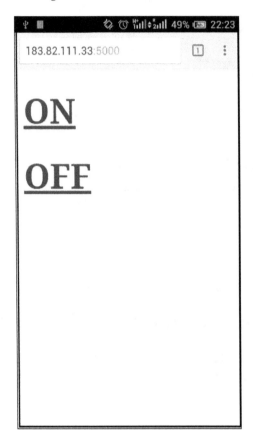

Now you can give the web link 183.82.111.33:5000 to any person who is connected to the Internet to access you BeagleBone board and control the bulb from any place around the world. Thus, you have your home automation system connected to the Internet. You can also call it as you have built your Internet of Things project by end of this chapter. Try it out on your own to control two appliances, change the style of the HTML webpage and add colors and control graphics to the webpage to learn and have more fun.

Summary

In this chapter, we learnt how web servers work to setup our own home automation system where an AC bulb is controlled from any place around the world via the Internet. In the process of building it we learnt how to set up a web server on a BeagleBone board using a Python-Flask web framework. Then we also learnt how to interface an AC circuit with a BeagleBone board using a relay circuit to control an AC bulb via the web server running on the BeagleBone board. In this way, you have built an advanced Internet of Things project in this chapter. In the next chapter, we will be looking at how to interface a camera with the BeagleBone Black and work with OpenCV for image processing on BeagleBone Black.

7
Working with Images Using Computer Vision

In this chapter, we will be getting started on interfacing a USB camera with a BeagleBone board and capturing images from the camera using OpenCV. We will start by installing OpenCV first and then move ahead with capturing images using OpenCV and Python.

We will look deeply into the topics given in this chapter:

- Prerequisites
- Adding a USB camera to BeagleBone Black
- An introduction to OpenCV
- Using Python and OpenCV together
- Image capture from a camera using Python and OpenCV

Prerequisites

This topic will cover what parts you will need in this chapter. These can be bought online.

We will need the following materials to begin:

- 1x BeagleBone Black
- 1x microSD card with the latest version of Debian flashed on it to boot the BeagleBone board from a microSD card
- 1x 5V DC, 2A power supply
- 1x Ethernet cable
- 1x USB camera

Materials needed

- 1x BeagleBone Black
- 1x microSD card with latest version of Debian flashed on it to boot the BeagleBone board from an microSD card
- 1x 5V DC, 2A power supply
- 1x Ethernet cable
- 1x USB camera

Adding a USB camera to a BeagleBone board

Adding a USB camera to a BeagleBone board is pretty straightforward. All you need to do is get a USB camera that is compatible with Linux, so one which has drivers for Linux. These days almost all USB web cameras come with this support. If you have a very old USB web camera that you want to interface with a BeagleBone board, you might have to add some additional steps to install the device drivers to see your video camera element on the Linux devices list on the BeagleBone board. For this topic explanation, I used a Logitech C270 HD webcam, as shown in the following figure:

You can use the USB port available on the BeagleBone board to connect the USB camera as shown in the following picture:

Boot the BeagleBone board using Debian on the MicroSD Card that we flashed earlier, and login into the BeagleBone board via SSH. Now type the command `Lsusb` as shown in the following screenshot:

```
debian@beaglebone: ~                                          —    □    ×
login as: debian
Debian GNU/Linux 7

BeagleBoard.org Debian Image 2015-11-12

Support/FAQ: http://elinux.org/Beagleboard:BeagleBoneBlack_Debian

default username:password is [debian:temppwd]

debian@192.168.1.20's password:
Last login: Fri Jan 29 15:44:49 2016 from 192.168.1.4
debian@beaglebone:~$ ls
Desktop  WorkSpace  bin
debian@beaglebone:~$ lsusb
Bus 001 Device 002: ID 046d:0825 Logitech, Inc. Webcam C270
Bus 001 Device 001: ID 1d6b:0002 Linux Foundation 2.0 root hub
Bus 002 Device 001: ID 1d6b:0002 Linux Foundation 2.0 root hub
debian@beaglebone:~$ 
```

If you are able to see the webcam listed on the device list, it means the camera is connected properly to the BeagleBone board, via USB.

Then, check whether the drivers are available for the camera in the Linux kernel and if it has successfully interfaced, and created a video input element in the list of devices in Debian. Let's change the directory to dev directory `cd /dev`, and then `ls`. If you see the **video0** listed on the list, then you can assume that everything went well and the USB web camera was interfaced with the BeagleBone board successfully. We now have a video0 element that we can use in OpenCV or in any other software that we will be installing in BeagleBone board to get a video input from the camera.

```
debian@beaglebone:~$ cd /dev/
debian@beaglebone:/dev$ ls
alarm               log_system          ptp0      tty12  tty41  ttyS2
ashmem              logibone_mem        pts       tty13  tty42  ttyS3
audio               loop-control        ram0      tty14  tty43  ubi_ctrl
audio1              loop0               ram1      tty15  tty44  uinput
autofs              loop1               ram10     tty16  tty45  urandom
binder              loop2               ram11     tty17  tty46  usbmon0
block               loop3               ram12     tty18  tty47  usbmon1
btrfs-control       loop4               ram13     tty19  tty48  usbmon2
bus                 loop5               ram14     tty2   tty49  v4l
char                loop6               ram15     tty20  tty5   vcs
console             loop7               ram2      tty21  tty50  vcs1
core                mapper              ram3      tty22  tty51  vcs2
cpu_dma_latency     media0              ram4      tty23  tty52  vcs3
disk                mem                 ram5      tty24  tty53  vcs4
dri                 mixer               ram6      tty25  tty54  vcs5
dsp                 mixer1              ram7      tty26  tty55  vcs6
dsp1                mmcblk0             ram8      tty27  tty56  vcs7
fb0                 mmcblk0p1           ram9      tty28  tty57  vcsa
fd                  mmcblk0p2           random    tty29  tty58  vcsa1
full                mmcblk1             root      tty3   tty59  vcsa2
fuse                mmcblk1boot0        rtc0      tty30  tty6   vcsa3
hwrng               mmcblk1boot1        shm       tty31  tty60  vcsa4
i2c-0               mmcblk1p1           snd       tty32  tty61  vcsa5
i2c-1               mmcblk1p2           sndstat   tty33  tty62  vcsa6
initctl             mqueue              stderr    tty34  tty63  vcsa7
input               net                 stdin     tty35  tty7   video0
kmem                network_latency     stdout    tty36  tty8   watchdog
kmsg                network_throughput  tty       tty37  tty9   watchdog0
log                 null                tty0      tty38  ttyGS0 xconsole
log_events          ppp                 tty1      tty39  ttyO0  zero
log_main            psaux               tty10     tty4   ttyS0
log_radio           ptmx                tty11     tty40  ttyS1
debian@beaglebone:/dev$
```

Now that we have a video component available in our BeagleBone board, we can go ahead and install OpenCV to get started with capturing images from the USB web camera and store them on the microSD card available on our BeagleBone board.

OpenCV – introduction and setting up on the BeagleBone board

In this topic you will learn about what OpenCV is and how we can use it to capture images from a web camera that is connected to the BeagleBone board.

OpenCV stands for Open Source Computer Vision. It is mainly designed for real-time computer visualization. So, this library will basically help us to use commonly used programming languages like C, C++ and Python to capture images from the camera connected to our computer – in our case, using the BeagleBone board. When we go to the project section of this chapter to capture an image from the USB camera using Python, you will understand how simple the OpenCV library makes it to code in getting inputs from the camera, generate outputs as image files, and much more in image processing.

Installing OpenCV on Debian on a BeagleBone board

Follow the steps to install OpenCV on Debian on a BeagleBone board:

Step 1: Install compiler:

```
sudo apt-get -y install build-essential cmake pkg-config
```

These compilers are very important to build packages from source codes and then install them. Installing them will be useful for us in future, particularly during the robot project:

```
debian@beaglebone:~/OCV$ sudo apt-get -y install build-essential cmake pkg-config
Reading package lists... Done
Building dependency tree
Reading state information... Done
build-essential is already the newest version.
cmake is already the newest version.
pkg-config is already the newest version.
0 upgraded, 0 newly installed, 0 to remove and 0 not upgraded.
debian@beaglebone:~/OCV$ []
```

Step 2: Install the other required packages that are needed before compiling compulsorily:

```
sudo apt-get install cmake git libgtk2.0-dev pkg-config libavcodec-dev
libavformat-dev libswscale-dev
```

In Linux, most of the software written will use other open source packages in them to build their software, so these packages are the ones that OpenCV use in their software to give us a beautiful and easy to code/use library.

```
debian@beaglebone:/dev$ sudo apt-get install cmake git libgtk2.0-dev pkg-c
onfig libavcodec-dev libavformat-dev libswscale-dev
Reading package lists... Done
Building dependency tree
Reading state information... Done
libgtk2.0-dev is already the newest version.
libgtk2.0-dev set to manually installed.
libavcodec-dev is already the newest version.
libavcodec-dev set to manually installed.
libavformat-dev is already the newest version.
libavformat-dev set to manually installed.
libswscale-dev is already the newest version.
libswscale-dev set to manually installed.
pkg-config is already the newest version.
git is already the newest version.
The following extra packages will be installed:
  cmake-data emacsen-common libxmlrpc-core-c3
The following NEW packages will be installed:
  cmake cmake-data emacsen-common libxmlrpc-core-c3
0 upgraded, 4 newly installed, 0 to remove and 0 not upgraded.
Need to get 5541 kB of archives.
After this operation, 11.6 MB of additional disk space will be used.
Do you want to continue [Y/n]? []
```

When you install the packages, if it prompts you to use additional disk space, go ahead and hit *Y* and then *Enter* to get started installing the required packages.

There are some more software packages you will have to install before compiling, which are listed following:

- `sudo apt-get -y install libjpeg62-dev`
- `sudo apt-get -y install libtiff4-dev libjasper-dev`
- `sudo apt-get -y install  libgtk2.0-dev`
- `sudo apt-get -y install libavcodec-dev libavformat-dev libswscale-dev libv4l-dev`
- `sudo apt-get -y install libdc1394-22-dev`
- `sudo apt-get -y install libxine-dev libgstreamer0.10-dev libgstreamer-plugins-base0.10-dev`
- `sudo apt-get -y install python-dev python-numpy`
- `sudo apt-get -y install libqt4-dev`
- `sudo apt-get install unzip`

Step 3: Install a few other optional softwares that might come in handy in the future while working with OpenCV. These are recommended by OpenCV:

- ```
  sudo apt-get install python-dev python-numpy libjpeg-dev
  libpng-dev libtiff-dev libjasper-dev libdc1394-22-dev
  ```

These softwares are not compulsory to for OpenCV to work, but when you connect a display to a BeagleBone board in the future and want to use graphics, these will surely come in handy. It's better to install them now instead of getting frustrated in the future with errors popping up when you write codes with display elements and GUI.

```
debian@beaglebone:/dev$ sudo apt-get install python-dev python-numpy libjpeg-dev libpng-dev libtiff-dev libjasper-dev
libdc1394-22-dev
Reading package lists... Done
Building dependency tree
Reading state information... Done
Note, selecting 'libjpeg8-dev' instead of 'libjpeg-dev'
Note, selecting 'libpng12-dev' instead of 'libpng-dev'
Note, selecting 'libtiff4-dev' instead of 'libtiff-dev'
libjasper-dev is already the newest version.
libjasper-dev set to manually installed.
libdc1394-22-dev is already the newest version.
libdc1394-22-dev set to manually installed.
libjpeg8-dev is already the newest version.
libjpeg8-dev set to manually installed.
python-dev is already the newest version.
python-numpy is already the newest version.
python-numpy set to manually installed.
libtiff4-dev is already the newest version.
libtiff4-dev set to manually installed.
libpng12-dev is already the newest version.
libpng12-dev set to manually installed.
0 upgraded, 0 newly installed, 0 to remove and 0 not upgraded.
```

By this stage, we have installed all the necessary packages needed to compile and install OpenCV on BeagleBone Black. So, now let's go ahead and download the source code files of OpenCV and then compile and install them. Let's create a new directory and save all the files inside it while building the OpenCV library:

Step 4: Create an OpenCVdirectory with the following commands:

- ```
  mkdir OCV
  ```
- ```
  cd OCV
  ```

It will look like this:

```
debian@beaglebone:~$ mkdir OCV
debian@beaglebone:~$ cd OCV
debian@beaglebone:~/OCV$ []
```
```

Step 5: Clone the OpenCV source code into our working directory:

- `wget https://sourceforge.net/projects/opencvlibrary/files/opencv-unix/2.4.9/opencv-2.4.9.zip`

The `wget` command will download the file from the URL that follows it and save it in the present working directory. You can see the percentage of the download status as it happens in the Linux shell, as shown in the following screenshot:

```
debian@beaglebone:~/OCV$ wget https://sourceforge.net/projects/opencvlibrary/files/opencv-unix/2.4.9/opencv-2.4.9.zip
--2016-02-17 05:44:52--  https://sourceforge.net/projects/opencvlibrary/files/opencv-unix/2.4.9/opencv-2.4.9.zip
Resolving sourceforge.net (sourceforge.net)... 216.34.181.60
Connecting to sourceforge.net (sourceforge.net)|216.34.181.60|:443... connected.
HTTP request sent, awaiting response... 302 Found
Location: https://sourceforge.net/projects/opencvlibrary/files/opencv-unix/2.4.9/opencv-2.4.9.zip/download [following]
--2016-02-17 05:44:56--  https://sourceforge.net/projects/opencvlibrary/files/opencv-unix/2.4.9/opencv-2.4.9.zip/download
Connecting to sourceforge.net (sourceforge.net)|216.34.181.60|:443... connected.
HTTP request sent, awaiting response... 302 Found
Location: http://downloads.sourceforge.net/project/opencvlibrary/opencv-unix/2.4.9/opencv-2.4.9.zip?r=&ts=1455687900&use_mirror=nchc [
--2016-02-17 05:45:01--  http://downloads.sourceforge.net/project/opencvlibrary/opencv-unix/2.4.9/opencv-2.4.9.zip?r=&ts=1455687900&us
Resolving downloads.sourceforge.net (downloads.sourceforge.net)... 216.34.181.59
Connecting to downloads.sourceforge.net (downloads.sourceforge.net)|216.34.181.59|:80... connected.
HTTP request sent, awaiting response... 302 Found
Location: http://nchc.dl.sourceforge.net/project/opencvlibrary/opencv-unix/2.4.9/opencv-2.4.9.zip [following]
--2016-02-17 05:45:02--  http://nchc.dl.sourceforge.net/project/opencvlibrary/opencv-unix/2.4.9/opencv-2.4.9.zip
Resolving nchc.dl.sourceforge.net (nchc.dl.sourceforge.net)... 211.79.60.17, 2001:e10:ffff:1f02::17
Connecting to nchc.dl.sourceforge.net (nchc.dl.sourceforge.net)|211.79.60.17|:80... connected.
HTTP request sent, awaiting response... 200 OK
Length: 91684751 (87M) [application/octet-stream]
Saving to: `opencv-2.4.9.zip'

38% [===================================>                                   ]
```

You need to wait until the download completes and check whether you received the zip file by using the `ls` command. If you see the file, as shown in the following screenshot, you can proceed to the next step:

```
Saving to: `opencv-2.4.9.zip'

100%[=======================================================================>] 91,684,751  3.61M/s

2016-02-17 05:45:27 (3.52 MB/s) - `opencv-2.4.9.zip' saved [91684751/91684751]

debian@beaglebone:~/OCV$ ls
opencv-2.4.9.zip
debian@beaglebone:~/OCV$
```

Step 6: Building OpenCV from source files using cmake:

- `unzip opencv-2.4.9.zip -d opencv`

First we need to unzip the `.zip` file we downloaded to extract the contents of the file.

```
debian@beaglebone:~/OCV$ unzip opencv-2.4.9.zip -d opencv
```

Then we compile the files inside it wait until unzipping process is completed:

```
  inflating: opencv/opencv-2.4.9/samples/winrt/OcvImageProcessing/OcvImageProcessing/OcvImageProcessing.vcxproj
  inflating: opencv/opencv-2.4.9/samples/winrt/OcvImageProcessing/OcvImageProcessing/OcvImageProcessing.vcxproj.filters
  inflating: opencv/opencv-2.4.9/samples/winrt/OcvImageProcessing/OcvImageProcessing/Package.appxmanifest
  inflating: opencv/opencv-2.4.9/samples/winrt/OcvImageProcessing/OcvImageProcessing/pch.cpp
  inflating: opencv/opencv-2.4.9/samples/winrt/OcvImageProcessing/OcvImageProcessing/pch.h
debian@beaglebone:~/OCV$
```

Then use the `ls` command to check whether an `opencv` folder is created and the contents of the `.zip` have been extracted inside it:

- `ls`

You can see the `opencv` folder has been created, inside which the files have been unzipped: `cd opencv`:

```
debian@beaglebone:~/OCV$ ls
opencv  opencv-2.4.9.zip
debian@beaglebone:~/OCV$ cd opencv
debian@beaglebone:~/OCV/opencv$ []
```

This is how the `ls` and `cd opencv-2.4.9` will look like in the command:

```
debian@beaglebone:~/OCV/opencv$ ls
opencv-2.4.9
debian@beaglebone:~/OCV/opencv$ cd opencv-2.4.9
debian@beaglebone:~/OCV/opencv/opencv-2.4.9$ []
```

Now we need to create a folder inside which we will compile and build the files for installation from the source files available inside the `opencv-2.4.9` folder. You need to execute the commands `mkdir build` and `cd build` in order to do that:

```
debian@beaglebone:~/OCV/opencv/opencv-2.4.9$ mkdir build
debian@beaglebone:~/OCV/opencv/opencv-2.4.9$ cd build
debian@beaglebone:~/OCV/opencv/opencv-2.4.9/build$ []
```

- `cmake -D CMAKE_BUILD_TYPE=RELEASE -D CMAKE_INSTALL_PREFIX=/usr/ local -D WITH_TBB=ON -D BUILD_NEW_PYTHON_SUPPORT=ON -D WITH_ V4L=ON -D INSTALL_C_EXAMPLES=ON -D INSTALL_PYTHON_EXAMPLES=ON -D BUILD_EXAMPLES=ON -D WITH_QT=OFF -D WITH_OPENGL=ON`

This is how it looks:

```
debian@beaglebone:~/OCV/opencv/opencv-2.4.11/release$ sudo cmake -D CMAKE_BUILD_TYPE=RELEASE -D
CMAKE_INSTALL_PREFIX=/usr/local -D WITH_V4L=ON -D WITH_GSTREAMER=ON -D WITH_OPENEXR=ON -D WITH
UNICAP=ON -D BUILD_PYTHON_SUPPORT=ON -D INSTALL_C_EXAMPLES=ON -D INSTALL_PYTHON_EXAMPLES=ON -D
BUILD_EXAMPLES=ON ..
```

Now, wait until the configuration is finished:

```
-- Configuring done
-- Generating done
-- Build files have been written to: /home/debian/OCV/opencv/opencv-2.4.9/build
debian@beaglebone:~/OCV/opencv/opencv-2.4.9/build$ []
```

Once it has finished, you should see something like the preceding screenshot.

Now we can go ahead and compile the files:

Step 7: Compile make and it will look like this:

```
debian@beaglebone:~/OCV/opencv/opencv-2.4.9/build$ make
[  0%] Generating opencv_core_pch_dephelp.cxx
Scanning dependencies of target opencv_core_pch_dephelp
[  0%] Building CXX object modules/core/CMakeFiles/opencv_core_pch_dephelp.dir/opencv_core_pch_dephelp.cxx.o
Linking CXX static library ../../lib/libopencv_core_pch_dephelp.a
[  0%] Built target opencv_core_pch_dephelp
Scanning dependencies of target pch_Generate_opencv_core
[  0%] Generating precomp.hpp
```

Wait until the program is compiled and ready to install:

```
[100%] Built target example_ocl_surf_matcher
Scanning dependencies of target example_ocl_tvl1_optical_flow
[100%] Building CXX object samples/ocl/CMakeFiles/example_ocl_tvl1_optical_flow.dir/tvl1_optical_flow.cpp.o
Linking CXX executable ../../bin/ocl-example-tvl1_optical_flow
[100%] Built target example_ocl_tvl1_optical_flow
debian@beaglebone:~/OCV/opencv/opencv-2.4.9/build$ []
```

Once the files are compiled and built, we can install OpenCV libraries to our system using the next step:

Step 8: Install sudo make install:

```
debian@beaglebone:~/OCV/opencv/opencv-2.4.9/build$ sudo make install
[  0%] Built target opencv_core_pch_dephelp
[  0%] Built target pch_Generate_opencv_core
[  3%] Built target opencv_core
```

Wait until the program is installed.

```
-- Installing: /usr/local/share/OpenCV/samples/ocl/adaptive_bilateral_filter.cpp
-- Installing: /usr/local/share/OpenCV/samples/ocl/bgfg_segm.cpp
debian@beaglebone:~/OCV/opencv/opencv-2.4.9/build$ []
```

Once installed let's go ahead and test whether everything was installed properly with the following command:

Step 9: Validate the installation

Since we will be using Python and OpenCV together, lets validate whether the Python library of OpenCV was installed properly or not, using the following command:

- `sudo python`

Inside the Python interactive shell enter the `from cv2 import _version_` command to import the library, and then to print the version execute the following command:

- `_version_`

You should see something like the following screenshot:

```
debian@beaglebone:~/OCV/opencv/opencv-2.4.9/build$ sudo python
Python 2.7.3 (default, Mar 14 2014, 17:55:54)
[GCC 4.6.3] on linux2
Type "help", "copyright", "credits" or "license" for more information.
>>> from cv2 import __version__
>>> __version__
'2.4.9'
>>> []
```

If it prints the version without any errors, everything is fine, you can see that its **2.4.9**, and that is the same version you downloaded as a zip file in step 5.

Now that we have the OpenCV library successfully installed we can go ahead to our next topic where we will be using Python and OpenCV together to capture an image from the USB video camera that we have plugged into our BeagleBone board.

Project: Image capture from a camera using Python and OpenCV

In this chapter we will be writing a code to capture an image from a camera and saving it in .jpg format using Python.

Let's first create a directory named `ImageCapture` inside which we can save the Python file in which we write the code, and where we can also save the image file that we capture:

- `mkdir ImageCapture`
- `cd ImageCapture`

It will look like the following screenshot:

```
debian@beaglebone:~/WorkSpace$ mkdir ImageCapture
debian@beaglebone:~/WorkSpace$ cd ImageCapture
debian@beaglebone:~/WorkSpace/ImageCapture$ []
```

- sudo nano TakePhoto.py

  Refer to the following image:

```
debian@beaglebone:~/WorkSpace/ImageCapture$ sudo nano TakePhoto.py
```

Now we can go ahead and start writing the code to capture an image from the camera and save it on the BeagleBone Black:

The simplest code possible to do this is given in the following screenshot:

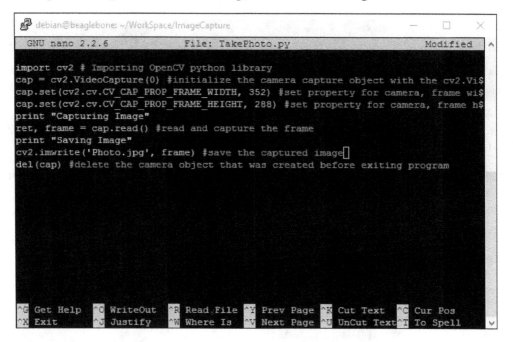

Save it and run it to capture an image from the camera and save it.

The output you will see when you run the code sudo python TakePhoto.py is as shown in the following screenshot:

```
debian@beaglebone:~/WorkSpace/ImageCapture$ sudo python TakePhoto.py
Capturing Image
Saving Image
```

If you don't get any errors and the program ends printing the **Saving Image** text, everything should have happened properly. To check this let's see whether the Photo.jpg file has been created inside the folder or not. You can use the ls command to do it and you should see the Photo.jpg file created as shown in the following screenshot:

```
debian@beaglebone:~/WorkSpace/ImageCapture$ ls
Photo.jpg   TakePhoto.py
```

Since we are working on BeagleBone Black via SSH we don't have the option to view the image directly on the GUI now – we will need a **File Transfer Protocol** (FTP) client software to download the image that was captured. So, let's go ahead and install one on our Windows PC now.

 FileZilla is my favourite, so I will be using it in this tutorial, you can use the ones you are familiar with or install FileZilla if you don't have it.

Once you have opened the FTP software, it will ask you for the IP address of the device, username, password, and port number:

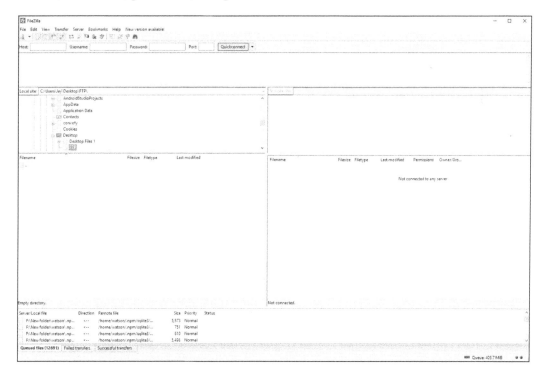

This is how the software looks. You can see on the top left corner a space for entering the host's IP address, username, password, and port number. Below that you can see the directory selection of where you want the files to be downloaded and uploaded from, and at the bottom, you can see the log of data transfers.

Now lets go ahead and connect our PC to the BeagleBone Black via FTP to transfer the image file we captured and see how it looks. The details you need to enter are the IP address assigned to the BeagleBone board, using which you connect to it via SSH, the same IP address and user name as debian and password temppwd which is default, if you have changed your username and password, then use them here and the port number is 22. Then click on the Quick connect button and you should see the files on the BeagleBone Black, as shown in the following screenshot:

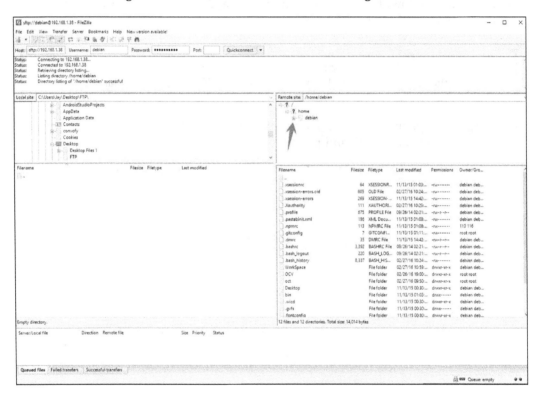

You can click on the + symbol next to the Debian folder shown in the picture and navigate to the ImageCapture folder inside which the Photo.jpg file that we captured and saved is present. You will see something like the following screenshot:

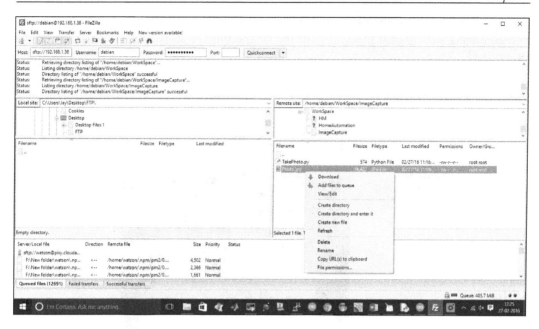

Now you can go ahead and download the file. Once you click on **Download**, the file will be downloaded to the FTP folder or the folder which you have selected on the PC fpr where the files will be downloaded. You can see in the following screenshot that the `Photo.jpg` file is now inside the FTP folder which was empty before on your PC:

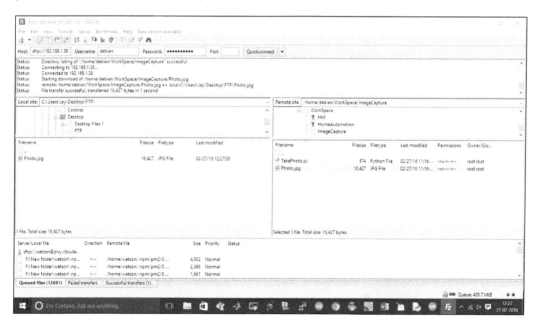

So, now that you have the photo that you captured, downloaded to your PC, you can go ahead and open it to see it with the image viewer software you have set up on your PC.

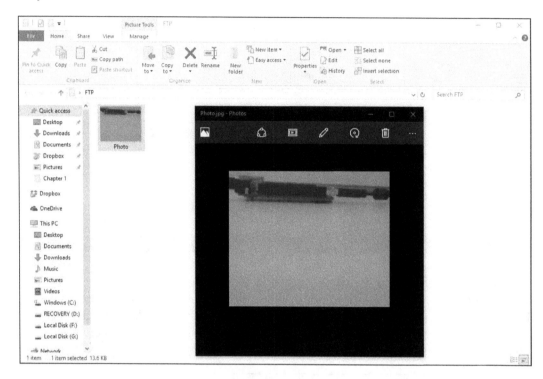

The image captured is as shown in the previous screenshot and the arrangement of the camera while taking this picture was as shown in the following screenshot:

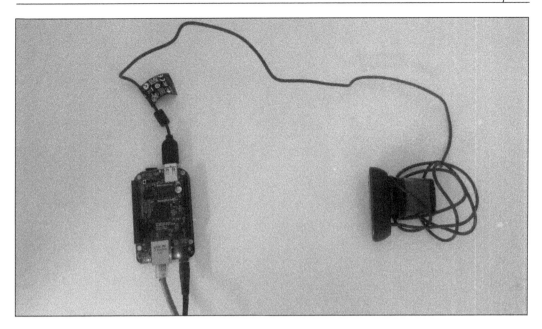

In the preceding picture you can see that the camera has been placed pointing towards the BeagleBone Black and at a distance, so the image that we captured was showing the side view of the BeagleBone Black, showing the USB connected to it, and the background.

So, in this way, you can use Python and OpenCV together to take pictures and save them for use in many applications.

Summary

This chapter was just a start for you get to know what open OpenCV is, to set it up on BeagleBone Black and to understand a little bit of what you can do with it using Python by writing just a few lines of code. In this chapter, the image capture project is just a simple thing we did – you can play around and do a lot more like capturing videos and saving them, changing a color image to black and white, and other image processing using OpenCV and Python. Now we know how to click a picture and save it.

In the next chapter, we will build a home security application project using a sensor to detect motion and click a picture whenever a motion is detected. In this way, we will be building a real-time application using OpenCV, BeagleBone Black and Python where the system will interact with the physical world.

8
Home Security Systems Using BeagleBone Black

In this chapter, we will focus on building a real-time Internet-connected home security surveillance system using the BeagleBone board. Similar to previous chapters, we will use OpenCV and Python on BeagleBone with a camera connected to it. But to take the project to an advanced level, we will add a PIR sensor to the BeagleBone board and write code on it to interact with the physical world. We will get started with motion detection using PIR sensors, followed by sending e-mails from BeagleBone boards using Python. We will finish the chapter with a project, in which we will build a motion-detection security camera that will send e-mail alerts with images captured whenever motion is detected by the PIR sensor.

The contents of this chapter are divided into the following topics:

- Prerequisites
- PIR sensors
- Motion detection using PIR sensors
- Sending e-mails with attachments
- Advanced project – motion detection, image capture, and alert system

Prerequisites

Here are the requirements:

- A BeagleBone Black
- A microSD Card with the latest version of Debian flashed on it to boot the BeagleBone board
- A 5V DC, 2A power supply
- An Ethernet cable
- A USB camera
- A PIR sensor

PIR sensors

A **PIR** (short for **passive infrared**) sensor is an electronic sensor that measures **infrared** (**IR**) light radiating from objects present in its field of view. Mostly, these sensors are used in PIR-based motion detectors.

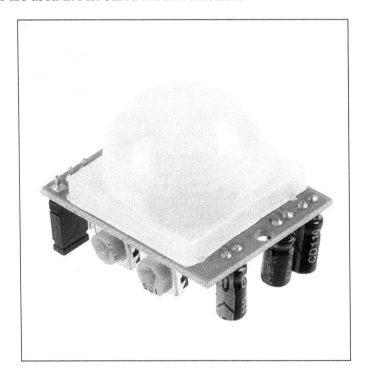

How PIR sensors work

If you look at the following diagram picture, a PIR sensor has two slots in it, and each slot is prepared with the help of special materials that are IR sensitive. The Fresnel lens helps the two slots in the sensor to widen the detecting area of the sensor as well as its distance, that is, the sensitivity of the sensor. Both slots detect the same amount of IR when there is no movement in front of the sensor or the detection area; we call this the idle state of the sensor, during which the slots detect the ambient amount of IR radiated from the room or outdoors. The sensor calibrates itself and waits for the movement of a warm body.

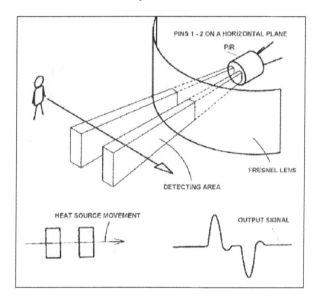

When half of the PIR sensor intercepts any warm body, such as a human or animal, it causes a positive differential change between the two halves of the PIR sensor. Similarly, a negative differential change is generated when the warm body leaves the sensing area, which is nothing but the reverse of the generation of a positive differential change. So, basically, the output we obtain is in the form of rising and falling pulses from the sensor output pin, using which we infer whether there was any movement in front of the PIR.

You might be wondering why there is a difference between the preceding diagram and the actual image of it, shown in the first image. Actually, the first image is to make you understand how the PIR sensor works. It shows the sensor available in market, which we will be using. In order to make the sensor work with a wide detection area, its lens is in the shape of a hemisphere, if you take a look at the following image, you can see that slots have been made at various angles on the lens to have a wide area of detection and for mounting at various places, such as ceilings and walls, to detect the motion of a moving body.

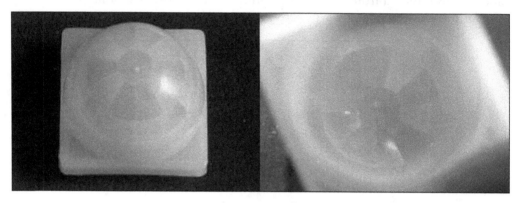

Most of these hobby-grade PIR sensors available in the market have a detection area 90 degrees wide, but some have one up to 110 degrees and 5 to 6 meters length. You can chose and buy whichever one you prefer.

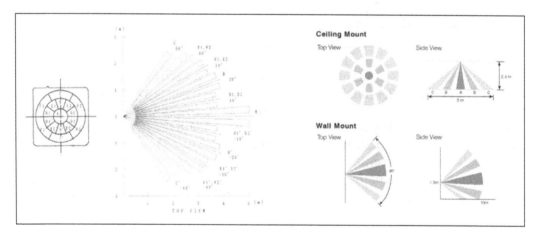

Motion detection using PIR sensors

Now that we know how a PIR sensors works, let's go ahead and hook it up with our BeagleBone board to detect motion.

First of all, take three berg wires and connect the PIR sensor to the BeagleBone board, as per the following circuit diagram:

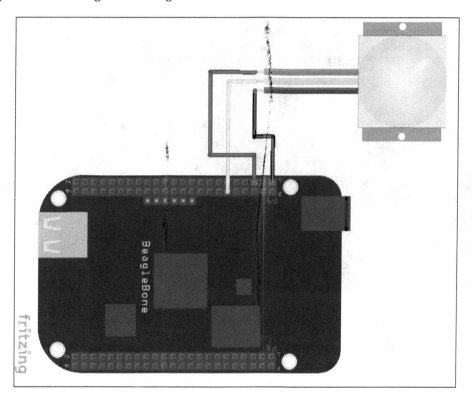

As shown in the preceding circuit diagram, connect the PIR sensor's Vcc to the 5V pin on the BeagleBone board, the output pin of PIR to GPIO60 on the BeagleBone board, and the ground pins on both with each other.

Then, we will turn on the BeagleBone board and log in to the Linux shell to start coding it.

Create a new Python program using `sudo nano TestPIR.py`:

```
debian@beaglebone:~/WorkSpace$ sudo nano TestPIR.py
```

Type in the code shown in the following screenshot:

```
GNU nano 2.2.6                          File: TestPIR.py

import time #Import Time Module
import Adafruit_BBIO.GPIO as GPIO # Import Adafruit GPIO Library
GPIO.setup("P9_12", GPIO.IN) # Setup GPIO60 / P9_12 as Input Pin
GPIO.add_event_detect("P9_12", GPIO.RISING) # Create a event to detect Rising pulse on GPIO60

try:
    while True:
        if GPIO.event_detected("P9_12"): #If RISING event detected
            print "Movement Detected" #prints out text saying Movement Detected
        time.sleep(0.05) #loop every 50 miliseconds to not overburden the CPU

except KeyboardInterrupt:
    print "Keyboard Interrupt"
    GPIO.cleanup()
    print "GPIO Cleaned"



^G Get Help    ^O WriteOut    ^R Read File   ^Y Prev Page   ^K Cut Text    ^C Cur Pos
^X Exit        ^J Justify     ^W Where Is    ^V Next Page   ^U UnCut Text  ^T To Spell
```

Once you have typed in the code, you can go ahead and save it using *Ctrl + X*.

Have a look at the comments in the code to get an idea of how it works. We are setting up `GPIO_60` as `INPUT PIN`, reading the RISING edge from the output coming from the PIR sensor, and printing out text saying **Movement Detected** every time we read a RISING edge from the sensor on GPIO pin `60`.

When you run the command, you should see the following output:

```
debian@beaglebone:~/WorkSpace$ sudo python TestPIR.py
Movement Detected
Movement Detected
Movement Detected
```

You can place your hand or make any movement in front of the sensor, as shown in the following picture:

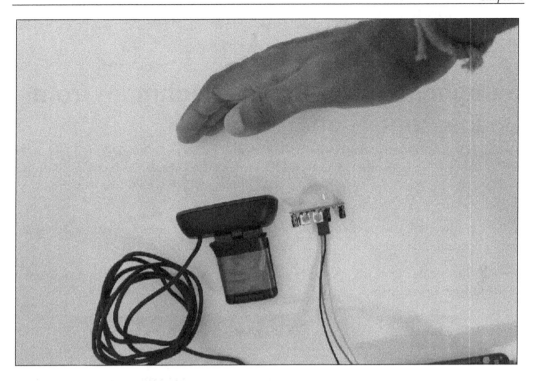

There is an option to set the sensitivity, that is, the range of the detection area, by varying the potentiometer on the sensor. Have a look at the following figure to get a better idea. You also have another potentiometer to vary the trigger time, which is nothing but the time period until which the pulse will be high and get back to low during the auto reset mode of the sensor. When it is set to no reset mode, the pulse will stay HIGH forever until another movement is detected. Usually, the preferred method is auto reset.

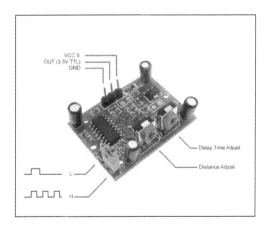

Now that we have tested the PIR sensors, let's move ahead to sending an e-mail with an attachment using Python from BeagleBone Black.

Sending e-mail with an attachment from BeagleBone Black

Like the OpenCV library to work with images and camera on BeagleBone Black with Python, we have many other wonderful libraries that are developed and are built in Python. One such library is the SMTP e-mail library, which we will be using in this section.

To test this, we will use the image we captured in the project in the previous chapter, available inside the `ImageCapture` folder.

We will change our working directory to the `ImageCapture` directory first, as shown in the following screenshot, using `cd ImageCapture`:

```
debian@beaglebone:~/WorkSpace$ cd ImageCapture
debian@beaglebone:~/WorkSpace/ImageCapture$
```

Then, we will go ahead and create a Python file with code to send an e-mail with an attachment in it. To do that, first create a new file named `sendemail.py`, using `sudo nano sendemail.py`:

```
debian@beaglebone:~/WorkSpace/ImageCapture$ sudo nano sendemail.py
```

Now, type in the code shown in the following screenshot and save the file inside the `ImageCapture` folder itself. The code has been written with comments on most of the lines for you to get a clear idea of how it works.

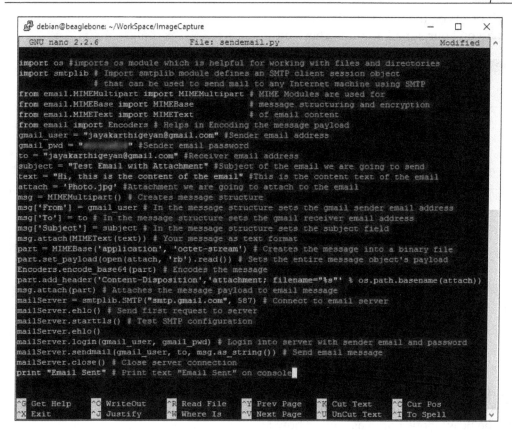

You'll see that the `Photo.jpg` file that we captured in our previous project is still available inside the `ImageCapture` folder, and it's the same image that we will be attaching in the e-mail that is going to be sent while executing this program:

```
debian@beaglebone:~/WorkSpace/ImageCapture$ ls
Photo.jpg   TakePhoto.py   sendemail.py
```

When you execute the program, you should get an e-mail on the receiver's e-mail address you mentioned in the `sendemail.py` code file, and the output the terminal will look like this:

```
debian@beaglebone:~/WorkSpace/ImageCapture$ sudo python sendemail.py
Email Sent
```

As it prints on the Linux shell that the e-mail was sent, you will have received the e-mail on your e-mail account; check out these screenshots of the e-mail I got:

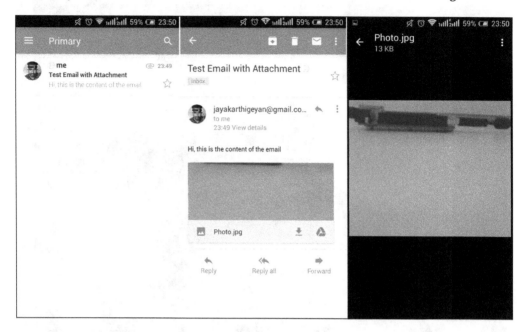

So, like this, you can attach any attachment to the e-mail and send it from BeagleBone. As we now know how to detect motion using a PIR sensor connected to the BeagleBone board as well as how to send an e-mail with a photo as an attachment, let's go ahead and merge the previous chapter's camera image-capture project with whatever we have learned so far in this chapter to build an advanced project.

Advanced project – Motion-based home security alert system

In this section, we will build a home surveillance security alert system, where we will have a BeagleBone board to which a PIR sensor is connected. A USB camera is connected to it, and the BeagleBone board is connected to the Internet. So basically, the system will capture an image from the camera whenever some movement is detected in front of the PIR sensor.

Follow these steps:

1. Set up the PIR sensor with the BeagleBone board, just like we did in the motion-detection topic of this chapter, connect the USB web camera to the BeagleBone board and, log in into the system. The setup looks as shown in the following picture:

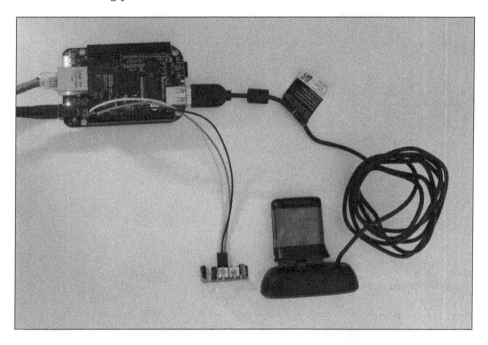

2. Create a new directory for this project with `sudo mkdir HomeSecurity`:

```
debian@beaglebone:~/WorkSpace$ sudo mkdir HomeSecurity
```

   Use `cd HomeSecurity`:

```
debian@beaglebone:~/WorkSpace$ cd HomeSecurity
debian@beaglebone:~/WorkSpace/HomeSecurity$
```

3. Create the Python script for the project using `sudo nano EmailAlert.py`:

```
debian@beaglebone:~/WorkSpace/HomeSecurity$ sudo nano EmailAlert.py
```

Type the following code into the file. The code contains comments on most of the lines to give you a clear explanation of how it works.

Once you have typed the code, go ahead and save it. When you run it, you should see the output in the Linux shell, as shown in the following screenshot, whenever there is movement in front of the PIR sensor:

```
debian@beaglebone:~/WorkSpace$ sudo python EmailAlert.py
Movement Detected
Capturing Image
Saving Image
Sending email
Email Sent
```

The following image shows how I waved my hand in front of the PIR sensor, keeping my finger in front of it and taking it away:

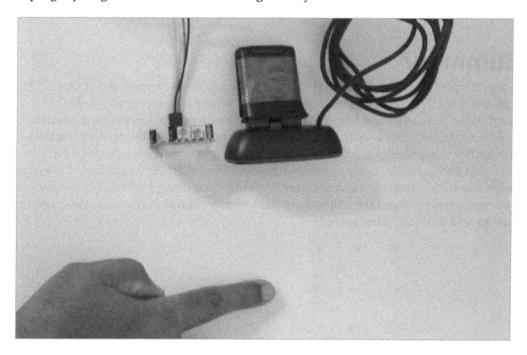

And the screenshots of the e-mail I got are shown in the following series of images:

Like this, you can use Python, OpenCV, and the e-mail library of Python together to click pictures and send an e-mail alert every time some movement is detected by the PIR sensor.

Summary

In this chapter, we used our knowledge from the previous chapter about OpenCV with what we learned in this chapter about PIR sensor interfacing using the BeagleBone board and sending e-mail using Python from the BeagleBone board to build a motion-detection camera surveillance security e-mail alert system. Instead of stopping this project here, I recommend you to try out other methods of motion detection and build the same system without a PIR sensor. There are lots of resources online on motion detection using OpenCV in real time using Python. Try setting up a system where without the PIR sensor, motion detection is performed using just the camera and an e-mail alert is sent.

9
Exploring Robotics

As the title says, we will be exploring and learning basic concepts of robotics in this chapter. We will begin with a basic introduction to robotics, with some definitions and explanations about robotics systems and a little bit of history about robots. Then, we will look into the robotics system structure, just like we did in *Chapter 3, Introduction to Physical Computing Systems*, regarding physical computing systems. We will take a look at the basic blocks of hardware and software involved in robotic systems, which is similar to our physical computing systems. Then, we will look into their operation, followed by differential drive robots at the end, because we will be building a differential drive robot in the next chapter.

The contents of the chapter are divided into the following sections:

- An introduction to robotics
- The elements, structure, and operation of robotics systems
- Application areas
- Differential-drive robots

Introduction to robotics

Many people remember only the famous actor Arnold Schwarzenegger and relate the humanoid terminator robot from the Terminator movies when they hear the word "robot". Even though it is true that the word robot relates to similar types of robots, people forget that the exact meaning of robots is not just that. Actually, that is just one type of robot: the humanoid type robots or—as people call them these days—androids are robots that resemble humans. We are still at the beginning stages of android robot development—there is a long way to go in that field of research if we are to reach results similar to science fiction movie robots.

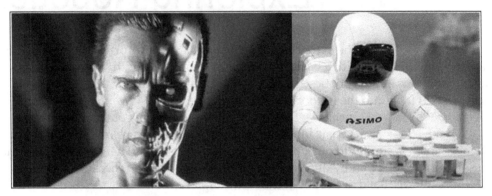

Sci-Fi humanoid robot versus the most advanced actual robot currently available

What is called a robot has many different definitions. The definitions depend on which technology is being used in the robotic system and what application the robotic system performs. Relating to the known definition of the physical computing system, we can define a robotic system as any physical computing system that is composed of electromechanical actuators that can either autonomously or semi-autonomously perform actions guided by a computer program running on its electronic hardware circuit.

A pick-and-place food robot and a hospital telepresence robot

In a much basic way, we can say that robots are machines that are designed in such a way that they are capable of carrying out one specific task or multiple tasks with speed and accuracy. You can easily buy many different types of robotic systems available in the market for different applications, starting from vacuum cleaner robots that clean your floors to robots that serve coffee and tea to you in a coffee shop and look exactly like a human being. We will discuss some of the widespread and current application areas of robots later in this chapter.

Even though robots have existed for a long time, they always used to be inside research labs and were costly for people to get until the industrial revolution. During the industrial revolution, manufacturers and industries wanted many industrial machines to speed up production and produce more items in less time without defects. Industrial machines started emerging, which were built from the structure of robotic systems such as robotic arms that were built using actuators and were capable of lifting heavy weights in the industries. In the early stages, almost all robotic systems were operated by humans using a remote control to ensure security and flexibility. But as software started becoming cheaper and more reliable, robotic systems with semiautonomous functions started to evolve, such as conveyer belts with robotic actuators that picked items from the conveyer and packed them automatically, and similarly, many other applications started to emerge in the industries. Nowadays, there are companies that manufacture food and beverages that are entirely prepared and packed by robots, with very little human intervention.

As a result of research and development to build smart and intelligent industrial robotic systems, many sensors and actuator mechanisms were developed to replace human intervention during production in industries, which led to the evolution of a wide variety of sensors that are not being developed further to build humanoid robots. Even though they showed such robots in movies more than a decade back, we still have many years to go until we build robots that can replace human beings.

Before we look into the wide application areas of robotic systems, let's look into the basic elements and structure of robotic systems in order to understand their functioning.

Elements, structure and operation of robotic systems

In this section, you will learn what the robotic systems are composed of, followed by their operation. Like we defined in the previous section, robotic systems are very similar to physical computing systems, just that in some physical computing systems, you might not have actuators that perform tasks that reduce human effort, unlike robotic systems. So, the elements of the systems as well as their operation are almost similar. In some cases, the term "physical computing systems" can be synonymous with robotic systems as well.

Just like any physical computing system, any robotic system will also have input sensors and output actuators connected to a CPU with input/output ports. The actuators are driven based on the computer program running on the CPU, which depends on the inputs from the sensors present in the robotic system.

To make it easy for you to understand as well as to give you a brief idea about the robot we will be building in the next chapter, let's take a look at the block diagram of a two-wheeled robot that will randomly move without hitting any surface:

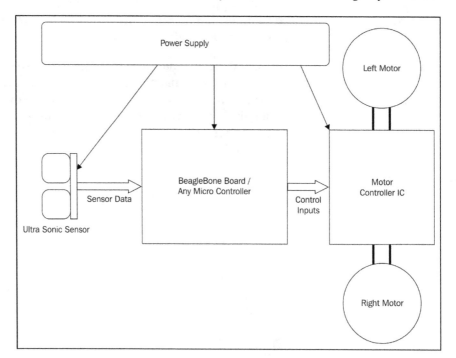

If you look at the block diagram, it consists of a sensor, that is, an **Ultra Sonic Sensor** that detects the distance of any obstacle in front of it from its position, and the sensor is connected to the input port of the CPU. Similarly, we have a **Motor Controller IC**, or the motor driver IC, which will help us drive heavy-duty motors with high voltages for them to run by taking digital inputs of low voltages that we get from the microcontroller. So, this motor driver IC is connected to the output port of the CPU. The motors are connected to the motor driver IC. Based on the inputs given to the motor driver IC, the motor is driven in a particular direction. We will look into this IC in detail in the next chapter. And, at last, the most important thing is that everything be powered using an external power supply, which is usually a DC source, but it can be AC sometimes, depending on the application. In our case, for the project in the next chapter, it will be DC. If you see the following block diagram of the physical computing system from *Chapter 3, Introduction to Physical Computing Systems*, you can understand that it is somewhat similar:

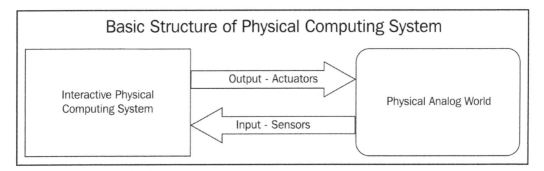

So, when you compare the structure with the structure of the robotic system we use for demonstrative purposes, it comprises a sensor that provides input to the CPU, and there is a driver IC that works depending on the output from the CPU to drive the motors. And in the CPU, we have software running that will randomly make the robot move without hitting any obstacle.

Depending on the software, the robot can operate in any way. For example, for a random obstacle-avoidance and autonomous robot that moves randomly, it moves the robot in the forward direction based on the outputs from the output pins of the microcontroller, and at the same time, the software keeps reading the distance measured by the ultrasonic sensor. Whenever an obstacle is detected at a set distance from the sensor, it is programmed to consider it as an obstacle. So, the program stops the motors from running by changing the output signal on the output pins of the controllers and then turns the robot either left or right. This can be random, or we can instruct it in our code to go only left or right every time an obstacle is detected. So, the robot starts to turn in a particular direction until there is free space for it to move and then stops again and starts moving straight. In this way, the program loop will be running and the robot will be moving randomly without hitting anything. This can sound dumb as it doesn't do any specific work nor performs any complex task. But when you add some more sensors to the system, such as a compass to read the angles at which it is starting to turn and some wheel encoders added to measure the distance travelled by the robot, and then write a program in such a way that it doesn't repeat travelling in the same area, it can become an awesome robot if you mount a vacuum cleaner system to it. One such robot is a commercially available vacuum cleaner robot.

So, any machine turns into a robot depending on how smart it works and solves a real-time problem and performs the action. Let's look into such examples, where robots with simple hardware but great software are being used in different applications, in the next section. Then, in the end, we will come back and look at differential-drive robots a little deeper to understand how actually these motors turn in different directions based on the motor directions using just two wheels with motors.

Application areas

When we discuss the application areas of robotics, we can see that the existence of robots is widespread. The most commonly categorized robotic systems based on application areas are as follows:

- Industrial robots
- Household or domestic robots
- Medical robots
- Mobile robots
- Social and humanoid robots

Industrial robotics

As mentioned before, even though we have been building robots for a long time, their widespread usage came about only through industrial robots in manufacturing to increase productivity. These are machines that perform specific tasks in industries at high speed.

In the preceding picture, you can see robotic arms manufacturing cars in a car manufacturing industry. The programming of these arms is done in such a way that all the robotic arms and conveyers that are moving the cars work in a synchronous way and each of these robot arms perform a specific task, such as fitting a nut or welding two metal sheets.

Domestic robots

Robots that help humans with household chores are called domestic robots. The first one of the following is a fictional domestic robot:

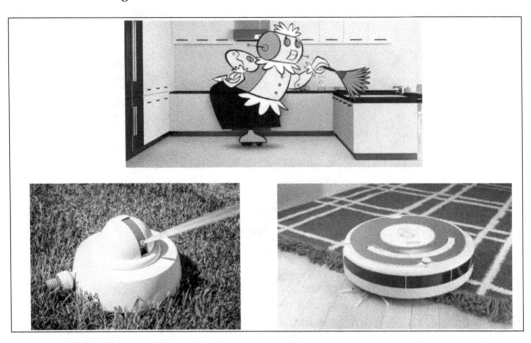

https://glennhsmith.files.wordpress.com/2013/04/rosie-the-robot-h.jpg

http://static01.nyt.com/images/2014/12/25/garden/20141225-TECH-slide-3TZF/20141225-TECH-slide-3TZF-jumbo.jpg

https://s.yimg.com/ny/api/res/1.2/HUZ5Rw7cnzK2z_k8zuI5ZA--/YXBwaWQ9aGlnaGxhbmRlcjtzbT0x03c9NTc0O2g9NDM2O2lsPXBXBsYW51/http://boygeniusreport.files.wordpress.com/2014/02/roomba-robot-vacuum-cleaner.jpg

The bottom-left image of the preceding composite shows a robot that waters your lawn every day at regular intervals of time, and the bottom-right image shows a vacuum-cleaning robot that cleans your house floor. I guess now you can relate it to the randomly working moving robot avoiding obstacles we discussed in the previous section.

Medical robotics

In recent times, surgical and rehabilitation robots are being used in the medical industry. As the names suggest, surgical robots helps doctors in performing complex surgeries, and rehabilitation robots help people get back use of their hands, arms, or any part of their bodies that have been replaced or become nonfunctional.

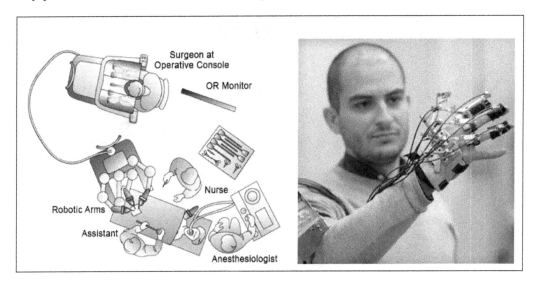

http://www.tipoist.com/indexfoto/robotic-surgery.jpg
http://www.salford.ac.uk/__data/assets/
image/0003/370434/dexterous-robot-hand-robotics-cse.jpg

If you look at the diagram on the left, you can see how a surgery is being performed using robotic arms: the surgeon operates the robotic arms looking at the console with the cameras on the arms and performs the surgery from the console. Just like I mentioned before, most robots are remotely operated. In many situations, with these robots, surgeons perform surgeries while in a different location from where the patients are.

If you look at the image on the right, it shows a man with an exoskeleton hand, and he has no thumb. But with the exoskeleton, he has a complete hand that can help him. These are nothing but robots that help with the rehabilitation of a human body part.

Mobile robots

Robots that can navigate and perform tasks are called mobile robots. There are many autonomous and semiautonomous robots that navigate and perform tasks, unlike fixed robotic arms that are used in industries and fixed lawn-watering robots in homes.

```
https://static-ssl.businessinsider.com/image/55d233c4
2acae700448be4de-960-720/to-make-things-a-bit-easier-
for-its-workers-amazon-added-about-15000-kiva-robots-
to-10-us-fulfillment-centers-during-the-2014-holiday-
season-amazon-bought-kiva-systems-the-company-that-
manufactures-the-robots-for-775-million-in-2012.jpg
https://cnet4.cbsistatic.com/img/g2VlwBmVinTwCSSQd2
BgrErY2Ws=/570x0/2016/03/18/6cdc953e-563b-4424-bf33-
6014b300e428/dominos-dru-pizza-robot-lifestyle.jpg
```

Take a look at the preceding images. The image on the left shows warehouse-management mobile robots that carry racks with items on them in a warehouse, depending on requests from the control unit. These robots are mobile and work much faster than humans going in search of a particular item and bringing it to the packing station or any place in the warehouse. These mobile robots have changed warehouse management drastically recently. Next, if you look at the image on the right side, it shows one of the latest mobile robots, which carries pizzas to its customers' home addresses and delivers them. These robots avoid obstacles and don't hit humans; they plan their path and keep moving. Vacuum-cleaner robots also come under mobile robots, but then again, they can be categorized as domestic robots, depending on their applications. So, most of these application areas are interlinked.

Mobile robots include even robots used in military applications, space exploration, under water robots, and so on.

```
https://s-media-cache-ak0.pinimg.com/236x/2d/ff/8d/2df
f8d05cf7f5ca90e6d4ab61148349d.jpg
http://i4.mirror.co.uk/incoming/article4822277.ece/
ALTERNATES/s615b/Curiosity-Rover.jpg
http://seahack.org/wp-content/uploads/2013/05/openrov_
large.jpg
```

If you look at the preceding images, you can see three different robots. The leftmost one is a military robot equipped with a weapon that can be triggered from a remote location. In the middle, we have the Mars rover, a robot that was sent to Mars to explore the planet's surface. It has a communication link with a station on Earth through satellites. And at last, to the far right, we have a robot that is used in underwater exploration, called the OpenROV. Now, an interesting fact about this robot is that it has been built with BeagleBone Black as the master controller in it. This is a prime example of how a hobby project using BeagleBone Black can be turned into a commercial product. We will also be building something similar in the next chapter. But instead of going underwater, it will explore what is around on the ground with a camera and show a live video feed to us.

From these examples, you can understand that even though they perform so many applications, the basic structure of these robots remains the same, and it's the add-on features that we give them using different sensors, actuators, communication links, and the software programs we write that make all the difference and give so many different names to the robots based on their applications.

Social and humanoid robots

Robots that resemble humans in look as well as interaction are called humanoid robots. Social robots are a specific group of these robots that don't have limbs like humanoids but have software running on them to interact socially like humans.

The following pictures show two robots that might help you differentiate between a humanoid and social robot:

http://letsmakerobots.com/files/imagecache/robot_
fullpage_header/field_primary_image/asimo.jpg
http://www.laptopreleasedate.com/wp-content/
uploads/2016/06/Robot-ASUS-Zenbo.jpg

If you look at the picture on the left-hand side, you can see a robot that looks like a human being with hands, legs, ears, and a face on a display. The robot is a great work of research and development in robotics, and it tries to resemble the human body's structure, with fingers on the hands to grab something and hold it and feet to walk from place to place. It also understands speech and responds to humans.

If you look at the image on the right, it shows one of the latest social robot that interacts with people based on voice processing. But this doesn't look like a human. Social robots are primarily built to work as personal assistants to humans. They're also meant for entertainment; for instance, the robot can tell you stories, play a song for you, and much more. I guess now you can understand why the "social" moniker is being given to such robots.

The categories and application areas of robots are endless. One book is not enough to explain all of it. You can do your own research to learn more. With that, we will end this topic and move on to differential-drive robots, which are one form of mobile robots, as this control mechanism is going to help us build our own mobile robot in the next chapter.

Differential-drive robots

Differential-drive is a control mechanism that is being used in most situations requiring control of navigating robots, especially for indoor applications. For beginners as well, this is considered the best control mechanism to get started with robots. Most indoor navigating robots used in industries and homes use this very mechanism.

The concept of this mechanism is to use two separately driven motors coupled with the wheels of the robot, separated by a distance and placed on a fixed common horizontal axis. The base also includes one or multiple caster wheels or roller-ball wheels attached to it to maintain equilibrium.

Here is how it looks:

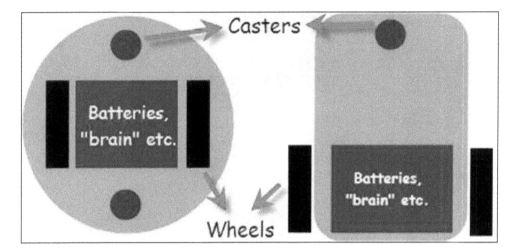

In the diagram, you can see two different configurations of differential-drive robots. The one on the left has two casters, while the other has just one. These two are one of the most commonly used differential-drive system configurations used. Both of them have different kinematics during navigation. If you want to look into it, you can read more on the Internet. Right now, to get started, you can chose one of these chassis—whichever you get in your market. The operation depends on controlling two motors using a motor driver IC and the outputs from the MCU.

When we look at the operation of these robots for navigation, it looks like these diagrams:

- Moving forward:

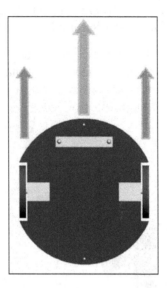

When the right-hand motor rotates clockwise and the left-hand one runs anticlockwise, the robot will move forward.

- Moving backwards:

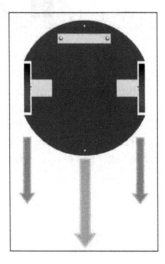

When the right-hand motor rotates anticlockwise and the left-hand one motor runs clockwise, exactly opposite to the directions during forward motion, the robot will move backwards.

- Turing left:

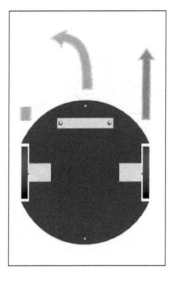

When the left-hand motor is stopped and the right-hand motor runs clockwise, the robot turns left.

- Turning right:

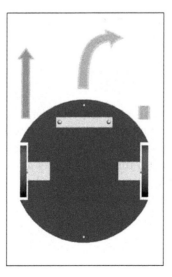

When the left-hand motor runs anticlockwise and the right-hand motor is stopped, the robot turns right.

- Spinning:

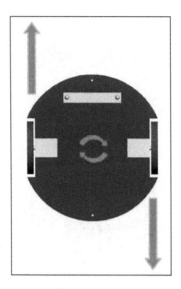

When both motors run in the anticlockwise direction, the robot spins clockwise on its own axis when looked at from above. Similarly, when the motor directions are reversed, it will spin anticlockwise.

- Stop:

I believe we don't need a picture to explain this action—if neither motor is running, the robot stops.

Summary

With that, we are at the end of this chapter, where we had a basic introduction to robotics, including some examples relating science fiction and reality, followed by a brief explanation of how robotic systems are structured and how they work. We also looked at some examples and discussed application areas. In the end, we also saw how differential-drive robots work and how they can be operated. We will be building our own live-video streaming differential-drive robot in the next chapter.

10

Building Your Own Robot

In this chapter we will see how to build our own robot using BeagleBone Black with Motors and Motor Driver IC interfaced with it. First we will learn about DC motors, followed by the L293D motor driver IC that will help us drive the DC motors. Then we will see how we can stream live video on a web page from the camera connected to the BeagleBone board. At the end we will build our own telecontrolled robot that you can control from a web page with a live video feed streaming from the camera connected to the BeagleBone Black.

The contents of this chapter are divided into:

- Prerequisites
- DC motors and the L293D motor driver IC
- Live video streaming on the BeagleBone board
- Advanced Project: A tele-controlled robot with live video streaming

Prerequisites

This topic will cover the parts you will need to get started with building the robot. These materials can be purchased from your local electrical hobby store or by ordering online from websites like Adafruit, Sparkfun, Seed Studio and so on.

Materials Needed
- 1x BeagleBone Black
- 1x microSD card with latest version of Debian flashed on it to boot the BeagleBone board from a microSD card
- 1x 5V DC, 2A power supply/mobile power bank with USB output of 5V 2A or more

- 1x USB WiFi dongle
- 1x BreadBoard
- 2x DC motors 50 to 100 RPM range operating at 12V
- 1x L293D motor driver IC
- 1x USB camera
- 1x USB hub
- 1x 12V or 9V battery
- 1x USB cable
- 1x DC barrel jack
- Connecting wires

DC motors

A DC motor is a motor that runs using a DC power supply.

As shown in the preceding picture, it has two terminal wires. We can call one of these terminal wire positive and the other one negative. Usually, these wires are marked red and black where red is positive and black is negative. Although these wires are marked positive and negative, unlike the battery, where these polarities can't be mixed, here in the DC motors they can be mixed.

Say, for example, on a motor, if the positive wire is connected to the positive terminal of the battery and the negative wire is connected to the negative terminal of the battery, or the power source, the motor rotates in a clockwise direction. When you reverse the connection, say from the positive terminal of the motor to the negative terminal of the battery and the negative terminal of the motor to the positive terminal of the battery, then the motor will rotate in an anti-clockwise direction, as shown in the following picture:

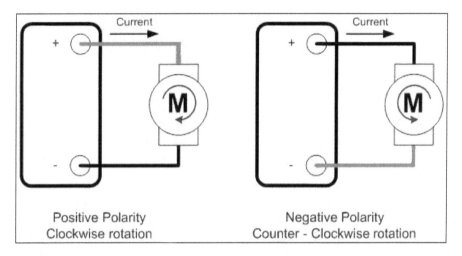

While the polarity of the voltage source's connection to terminals of the motor controls the DC motor's direction of rotation, the magnitude of the DC voltage source determines the speed of it.

But changing the polarity and switching the circuit on and off every time manually can be hectic job, and we need an electronic circuit that can help us do this without having to physically switch the connections. This is where motor driver ICs will come in useful to complete the task with digital inputs. One such motor driver IC is the L293D which will be discussing next.

L293D motor driver IC

As we mentioned previously, the L293D can be defined as a, H-Bridge motor driver circuit, which is made into a IC allowing us to drive a DC motor in either direction using digital inputs.

The pin configuration of the **L293D** is as shown in the following picture:

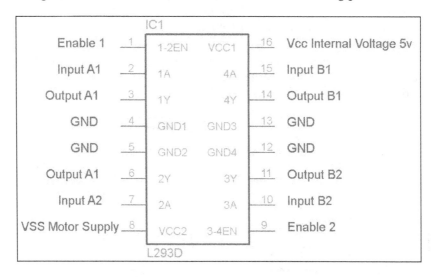

As shown in the preceding picture, in the L293D there are four input pins and four output pins. The two input pins, pin two and seven regulate the rotation of the motor connected to output pins three and six. Similarly, the input pins on the right, pin fifteen and ten regulate the rotation of the motor connected to output pins eleven and fourteen. The enable pins one and two, on the left and the right side of the IC on pin one and nine of the IC enables the operation of the output based on the input on that side of the IC. The motors rotate based on the inputs provided across the input pins as Logic 0 and Logic 1. Supply **5V** to the **Vcc** pin of the IC for its operation, and connect the ground pins to the ground and negative pins of the power supply. And finally, you need to connect the positive of the DC power source/battery to the **Vss** pin to provide a power supply to the motor, and connect the negative of the power supply to the **GND** pin.

Consider the circuit connection as shown in the following picture:

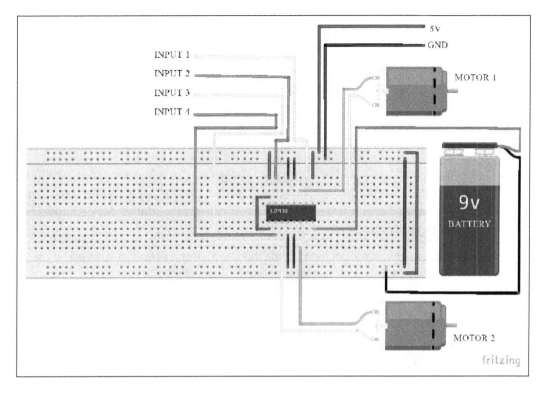

For the circuit shown previously, when input 1 is LOW and input 2 is HIGH, the motor 1 will rotate in a clockwise direction, similarly when both inputs 1 and 2 are LOW or HIGH the motor will not rotate. This can be explained using a logic table:

Input 1	Input2	Motor 1 Running Direction
HIGH	LOW	ANTI-CLOCKWISE
LOW	HIGH	CLOCKWISE
HIGH	HIGH	IDLE – NO ROTATION
LOW	LOW	IDLE – NO ROTATION

Similarly for input 3 and input 4 the output will be as shown in the following table:

Input 3	Input4	Motor 2 Running Direction
HIGH	LOW	ANTI-CLOCKWISE
LOW	HIGH	CLOCKWISE
HIGH	HIGH	IDLE – NO ROTATION
LOW	LOW	IDLE – NO ROTATION

You can test it by connecting it to the BeagleBone Black by writing a similar Python code to our blink code or the home automation code that we tried in our previous chapters. With this knowledge, you will have a clear idea of the concept of how the L293D operates. You can look at the datasheet of the L293D IC to get more details about the specifications and ratings of the IC. You can get this datasheet provided by the IC manufacturer on the Internet.

We will use the same circuit interfaced with the BeagleBone board at the end of the chapter to the build the robot in our final project. Now let's go ahead and see how we can stream video live on the BeagleBone board using the USB camera connected to it.

Live video streaming on the BeagleBone board

To stream live video from Logitech HD webcam C270 USB camera, connected via local server to the BeagleBone board you need to have a software package that can do the job. But you also need to install some essential software before you download and compile the live video streaming software. Let's get started with the installation of the software packages by executing the following commands :

- ` sudo apt-get install imagemagick`

```
debian@beaglebone:~/WorkSpace$ sudo apt-get install imagemagick
Reading package lists... Done
Building dependency tree
Reading state information... Done
The following packages were automatically installed and are no longer required:
  libasound2-dev libavahi-client-dev libavahi-common-dev libcaca-dev libdbus-1-dev
  libdirectfb-extra libgl1-mesa-dev libglu1-mesa-dev libilmbase-dev
  libopencv-contrib2.3 libopencv-flann-dev libopencv-gpu-dev libopencv-gpu2.3
  libopencv-imgproc-dev libopencv-ml-dev libopencv-video-dev libopenexr-dev
  libpulse-dev libpulse-mainloop-glib0 libslang2-dev libts-dev mesa-common-dev
Use 'apt-get autoremove' to remove them.
The following extra packages will be installed:
  fonts-droid ghostscript gsfonts imagemagick-common libcupsimage2
  libdjvulibre-text libdjvulibre21 libexiv2-12 libgs9 libgs9-common libijs-0.35
  libjbig2dec0 liblcms1 liblensfun-data liblensfun0 liblqr-1-0 libmagickcore5
  libmagickcore5-extra libmagickwand5 libnetpbm10 libpaper-utils libpaper1
  libwmf0.2-7 netpbm poppler-data ufraw-batch
Suggested packages:
  ghostscript-cups ghostscript-x hpijs imagemagick-doc autotrace cups-bsd lpr
  lprng enscript gimp gnuplot grads hp2xx html2ps libwmf-bin mplayer povray
  radiance texlive-base-bin transfig xdg-utils exiv2 liblcms-utils poppler-utils
  fonts-japanese-mincho fonts-ipafont-mincho fonts-japanese-gothic
  fonts-ipafont-gothic fonts-arphic-ukai fonts-arphic-uming fonts-unfonts-core
  ufraw
The following NEW packages will be installed:
  fonts-droid ghostscript gsfonts imagemagick imagemagick-common libcupsimage2
  libdjvulibre-text libdjvulibre21 libexiv2-12 libgs9 libgs9-common libijs-0.35
  libjbig2dec0 liblcms1 liblensfun-data liblensfun0 liblqr-1-0 libmagickcore5
  libmagickcore5-extra libmagickwand5 libnetpbm10 libpaper-utils libpaper1
  libwmf0.2-7 netpbm poppler-data ufraw-batch
0 upgraded, 27 newly installed, 0 to remove and 87 not upgraded.
Need to get 19.4 MB of archives.
After this operation, 52.5 MB of additional disk space will be used.
Do you want to continue [Y/n]? y
```

When you are prompted to continue the operation, type Y, as shown at the end of the preceding screenshot, and hit Enter to continue and finish the installation:

- `sudo apt-get install libjpeg8-dev`

```
debian@beaglebone:~/WorkSpace$ sudo apt-get install libjpeg8-dev
Reading package lists... Done
Building dependency tree
Reading state information... Done
libjpeg8-dev is already the newest version.
libjpeg8-dev set to manually installed.
The following packages were automatically installed and are no longer required:
  libasound2-dev libavahi-client-dev libavahi-common-dev libcaca-dev libdbus-1-dev libdirectfb-extra
  libgl1-mesa-dev libglu1-mesa-dev libilmbase-dev libopencv-contrib2.3 libopencv-flann-dev libopencv-gpu-dev
  libopencv-gpu2.3 libopencv-imgproc-dev libopencv-ml-dev libopencv-video-dev libopenexr-dev libpulse-dev
  libpulse-mainloop-glib0 libslang2-dev libts-dev mesa-common-dev
Use 'apt-get autoremove' to remove them.
0 upgraded, 0 newly installed, 0 to remove and 87 not upgraded.
```

- `sudo apt-get install subversion`

```
debian@beaglebone:~/WorkSpace$ sudo apt-get install subversion
Reading package lists... Done
Building dependency tree
Reading state information... Done
The following packages were automatically installed and are no longer required:
  libasound2-dev libavahi-client-dev libavahi-common-dev libcaca-dev libdbus-1-dev libdirectfb-extra
  libgl1-mesa-dev libglu1-mesa-dev libilmbase-dev libopencv-contrib2.3 libopencv-flann-dev libopencv-gpu-dev
  libopencv-gpu2.3 libopencv-imgproc-dev libopencv-ml-dev libopencv-video-dev libopenexr-dev libpulse-dev
  libpulse-mainloop-glib0 libslang2-dev libts-dev mesa-common-dev
Use 'apt-get autoremove' to remove them.
The following extra packages will be installed:
  libneon27-gnutls libsvn1
Suggested packages:
  subversion-tools db5.1-util
The following NEW packages will be installed:
  libneon27-gnutls libsvn1 subversion
0 upgraded, 3 newly installed, 0 to remove and 87 not upgraded.
Need to get 2171 kB of archives.
After this operation, 5429 kB of additional disk space will be used.
Do you want to continue [Y/n]? y
```

Now that we have installed all the prerequite softwares, let's download and compile the video streaming software.

First create a separate directory in the home directory, and put the contents of the streaming software inside it:

- `mkdir mjpg`

```
debian@beaglebone:~$ mkdir mjpg
```

Now let us change our working directory to the directory we created:

- `cd mjpg`

```
debian@beaglebone:~$ cd mjpg
debian@beaglebone:~/mjpg$ []
```

Once you are in the `mjpg` directory, you can download the mjpg-streamer software package using the command given following from the URL mentioned in the command:

- `svn co https://svn.code.sf.net/p/mjpg-streamer/code/mjpg-streamer/ mjpg-streamer`

```
debian@beaglebone:~/mjpg$ svn co https://svn.code.sf.net/p/mjpg-streamer/code/mjpg-streamer/ mjpg-streamer
[]
```

Once you have downloaded it there will be aa `mjpg-streamer` folder created, inside which you will have the source code of the software. Let's go ahead and change the directory to that first:

- `cd mjpg-streamer`

```
debian@beaglebone:~/mjpg/mjpg-streamer$ ▯
```

Now our next step will be compile the software using the `make` command:

- `make`

```
debian@beaglebone:~/mjpg/mjpg-streamer$ make
gcc -D'SVN_REV="3:172"' -O2 -DLINUX -D_GNU_SOURCE -Wall    -c -o mjpg_streamer.o mjpg_streamer.c
gcc -D'SVN_REV="3:172"' -O2 -DLINUX -D_GNU_SOURCE -Wall    -c -o utils.o utils.c
gcc -D'SVN_REV="3:172"' -O2 -DLINUX -D_GNU_SOURCE -Wall    mjpg_streamer.o utils.o -lpthread -ldl -o mjpg_streamer
chmod 755 mjpg_streamer
make -C plugins/input_uvc all
make[1]: Entering directory '/home/debian/mjpg/mjpg-streamer/plugins/input_uvc'
gcc -c -O1 -DLINUX -D_GNU_SOURCE -Wall -shared -fPIC -o v4l2uvc.lo v4l2uvc.c
v4l2uvc.c: In function 'init_videoIn':
v4l2uvc.c:88:23: warning: variable 'currentHeight' set but not used [-Wunused-but-set-variable]
v4l2uvc.c:88:9: warning: variable 'currentWidth' set but not used [-Wunused-but-set-variable]
gcc -c -O1 -DLINUX -D_GNU_SOURCE -Wall -shared -fPIC -o jpeg_utils.lo jpeg_utils.c
gcc -c -O1 -DLINUX -D_GNU_SOURCE -Wall -shared -fPIC -o dynctrl.lo dynctrl.c
gcc -O1 -DLINUX -D_GNU_SOURCE -Wall -shared -fPIC -o input_uvc.so input_uvc.c v4l2uvc.lo jpeg_utils.lo dynctrl.lo
 -ljpeg
make[1]: Leaving directory '/home/debian/mjpg/mjpg-streamer/plugins/input_uvc'
cp plugins/input_uvc/input_uvc.so .
make -C plugins/output_file all
make[1]: Entering directory '/home/debian/mjpg/mjpg-streamer/plugins/output_file'
gcc -O2 -DLINUX -D_GNU_SOURCE -Wall -shared -fPIC -o output_file.so output_file.c
make[1]: Leaving directory '/home/debian/mjpg/mjpg-streamer/plugins/output_file'
cp plugins/output_file/output_file.so .
make -C plugins/output_udp all
make[1]: Entering directory '/home/debian/mjpg/mjpg-streamer/plugins/output_udp'
gcc -O2 -DLINUX -D_GNU_SOURCE -Wall -shared -fPIC -o output_udp.so output_udp.c
make[1]: Leaving directory '/home/debian/mjpg/mjpg-streamer/plugins/output_udp'
cp plugins/output_udp/output_udp.so .
make -C plugins/output_http all
make[1]: Entering directory '/home/debian/mjpg/mjpg-streamer/plugins/output_http'
gcc -c -O1 -DLINUX -D_GNU_SOURCE -Wall -shared -fPIC -o httpd.lo httpd.c
gcc -O1 -DLINUX -D_GNU_SOURCE -Wall -shared -fPIC -o output_http.so output_http.c httpd.lo
make[1]: Leaving directory '/home/debian/mjpg/mjpg-streamer/plugins/output_http'
cp plugins/output_http/output_http.so .
make -C plugins/input_testpicture all
make[1]: Entering directory '/home/debian/mjpg/mjpg-streamer/plugins/input_testpicture'
convert pictures/960x720_1.jpg -resize 640x480! pictures/640x480_1.jpg
convert pictures/960x720_1.jpg -resize 320x240! pictures/320x240_1.jpg
convert pictures/960x720_1.jpg -resize 160x120! pictures/160x120_1.jpg
converting file: 160x120_1.jpg
converting file: 320x240_1.jpg
converting file: 640x480_1.jpg
converting file: 960x720_1.jpg
converting file: 160x120_2.jpg
converting file: 320x240_2.jpg
converting file: 640x480_2.jpg
converting file: 960x720_2.jpg
gcc -O2 -DLINUX -D_GNU_SOURCE -Wall -shared -fPIC -o input_testpicture.so input_testpicture.c
make[1]: Leaving directory '/home/debian/mjpg/mjpg-streamer/plugins/input_testpicture'
cp plugins/input_testpicture/input_testpicture.so .
make -C plugins/input_file all
make[1]: Entering directory '/home/debian/mjpg/mjpg-streamer/plugins/input_file'
gcc -O2 -DLINUX -D_GNU_SOURCE -Wall -shared -fPIC  -o input_file.so input_file.c
make[1]: Leaving directory '/home/debian/mjpg/mjpg-streamer/plugins/input_file'
cp plugins/input_file/input_file.so .
```

Once you have successfully compiled the software without errors you can go ahead and run the software using the following command:

- `/mjpg_streamer -i "./input_uvc.so -d /dev/video0 -n -y" -o "./output_http.so -w ./www"`

If the Apache server is installed on your Debian package then it might show an error saying **bind: Address already in use** as shown in the following screenshot when you execute the preceding command to run the video streaming software:

```
debian@beaglebone:~/mjpg/mjpg-streamer$ sudo ./mjpg_streamer -i "./input_uvc.so -d /dev/video0 -n -y" -o "./output_http.so -w ./www"
MJPG Streamer Version: svn rev: 3:172
 i: Using V4L2 device.: /dev/video0
 i: Desired Resolution: 640 x 480
 i: Frames Per Second.: 5
 i: Format............: YUV
 i: JPEG Quality......: 80
 o: www-folder-path...: ./www/
 o: HTTP TCP port.....: 8080
 o: username:password.: disabled
 o: commands..........: enabled
bind: Address already in use
bind: Address already in use
```

This is due to port `8080` being used by default by the Apache server. In this case, to resolve the issue, we can change the port used by Apache to `8079`, or any other permited number as shown in the following screenshot, by changing the details in the `ports.conf` file:

- `sudo nano /etc/apache2/ports.conf`

```
debian@beaglebone:~/mjpg/mjpg-streamer$ sudo nano /etc/apache2/ports.conf
```

Once you open the file you can change the `NameVirtualHost` to `8079` and `Listen` to `8079` port as shown in the following screenshot and save it:

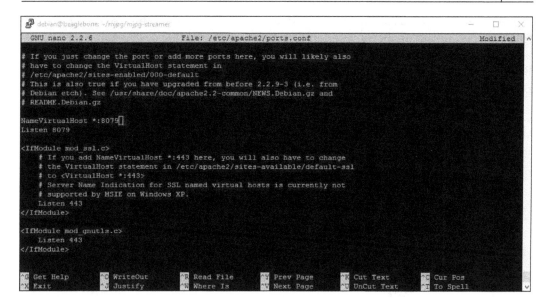

Once you save it, you need to restart the Apache server to perform the changes. To do that, execute the `service restart` command:

- `sudo service apache2 restart`

```
debian@beaglebone:~/mjpg/mjpg-streamer$ sudo service apache2 restart
[ ok ] Restarting apache2 (via systemctl): apache2.service.
debian@beaglebone:~/mjpg/mjpg-streamer$ []
```

Once you restart and get the output as shown in the preceding screenshot, it means the changes have been made. Now you can go ahead and run the streaming software by executing the following command:

- `sudo ./mjpg_streamer -i "./input_uvc.so -d /dev/video0 -n -y"`
  `-o "./output_http.so -w ./www"`

```
debian@beaglebone:~/mjpg/mjpg-streamer$ sudo ./mjpg_streamer -i "./input_uvc.so -d /dev/video0 -n -y" -o "./output_http.so -w ./www"
MJPG Streamer Version: svn rev: 3:172
 i: Using V4L2 device.: /dev/video0
 i: Desired Resolution: 640 x 480
 i: Frames Per Second.: 5
 i: Format............: YUV
 i: JPEG Quality......: 80
 o: www-folder-path...: ./www/
 o: HTTP TCP port.....: 8080
 o: username:password.: disabled
 o: commands..........: enabled
[]
```

If you see the output as shown in the previous screenshot, then the streaming software is running properly. We can test it by visiting the local server at port `8080` as shown in the following screenshot. The IP address is the IP address of the BeagleBone Black on your router, which is same as the one we used to login to the BeagleBone board.

Once you open the web link, you will see the streaming software's home webpage as shown on the next page:

The software description page with the details about which streaming software we are running on the BeagleBone board is shown in the previous screenshot. On the home page itself you can see the image captured from the camera but it's a static image which is not a live stream. To see the live stream, click on the **Stream** button on the left and it will show you the live streamed web page where you can see the live feed from the camera as shown in the following screenshot:

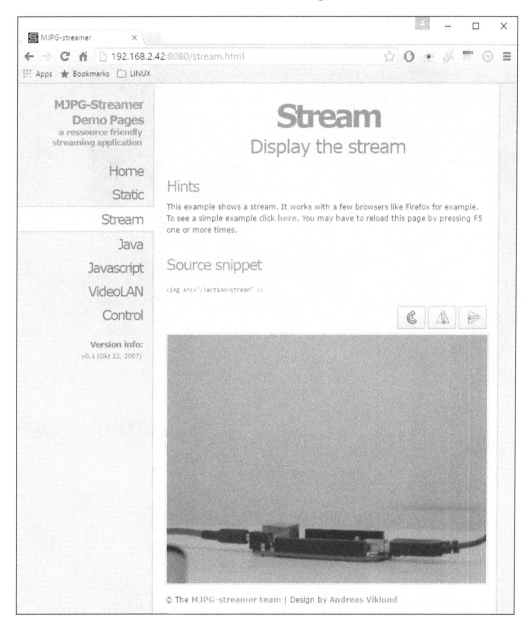

Click the button **here**, which is highlighted in red saying **To see a simple example click here**. You will see just the video feed separately as a image element on an HTML page as shown in the following screenshot:

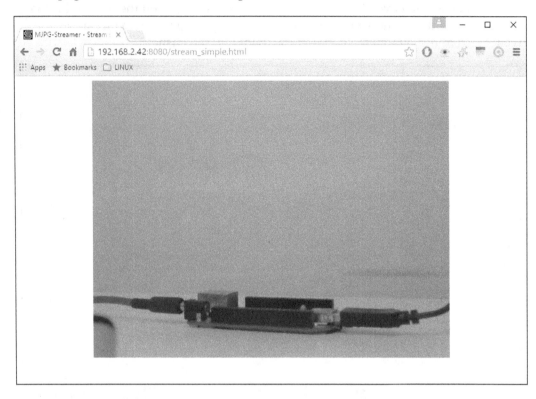

A setup of the BeagleBone board with the USB camera whilst the live feed is being streamed is shown in the following screenshot:

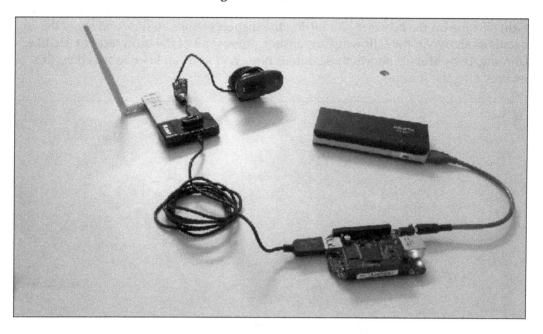

So, you can see that the BeagleBone and the power bank which are in front of the camera are visible on the live feed. If you just wave your hand in front of the camera you can see it live on the web page.

Now that we have seen the live video feed on this, if you want to include it on any HTML page you want to create, you can do so by adding the image source element created by the streaming software. You get the information of that image source by right clicking on the browser and hitting the inspect element which will show the details as shown in the following screenshot. Almost all of the browsers we use like Chrome, IE or Mozilla shows these details now, and you can learn more about this by browsing the Internet.

The image element can be identified on the inspection block on the right side of the browser window where the details is mentioned as shown in the preceding screenshot:

```
<img src="http://192.168.2.42:8080/?action=stream">
```

We will be using this in our project at the end of this chapter to get a live feed on the web page using a Flask framework and Python. Now that we know how to get a live feed from the USB camera and integrate it on a webpage, let's go ahead to the next topic in this chapter where we will be building a robot with live video streaming.

Advanced project – a telecontrolled robot with live video streaming

First connect the motor driver IC with motors, power supply as shown in the following circuit:

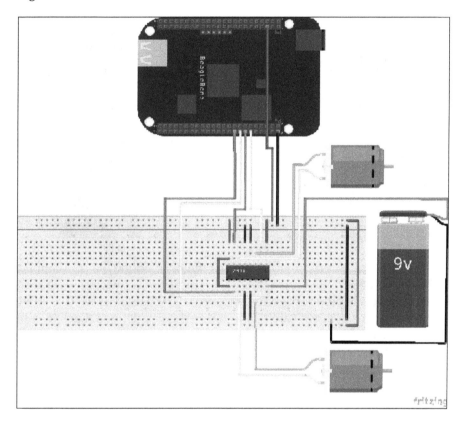

The whole setup will look like the following picture:

So you can see from the preceding picture that the BeagleBone Black is connected to a USB hub to which the WiFi dongle and USB camera are connected. Also the L293D is connected to motors of the robot and an external 12V battery is used to drive the motors. The input pins of L293D are connected to the BeagleBone Black to control the L293D. The BeagleBone Black is powered using a mobile power bank using a USB to DC barrel connector cable, which you can make on your own as shown in the following picture:

So why can't the BeagleBone board be powered using the inbuilt USB connection?. This is because the USB only draws 500mAh in total from the input supply, which isn't sufficient to power up the USB webcam and the Wi-Fi dongle.

Now, you can login into the BeagleBone Black and write the code to control the robot from the web page.

In this project, we will not be writing the code from scratch – instead we will be writing it by editing the code from our home automation project from *Chapter 6, Home Automation Using BeagleBone*. So let's go ahead to the home automation directory in the Linux shell after logging into it:

- `cd WorkSpace/HomeAutomation`

```
debian@beaglebone:~$ cd WorkSpace/HomeAutomation
debian@beaglebone:~/WorkSpace/HomeAutomation$
```

If you list the contents in the directory using the `ls` command, you will see the following:

```
debian@beaglebone:~/WorkSpace/HomeAutomation$ ls
ControlWebApp.py        WebApp.py               WebAppFromTemplate.py    templates
GPIOControlWebApp.py    WebAppButtonTest.py     control.py
debian@beaglebone:~/WorkSpace/HomeAutomation$
```

Once you are in the home automation directory, let's first edit the HTML template:

- `cd templates`

```
debian@beaglebone:~/WorkSpace/HomeAutomation$ cd templates
debian@beaglebone:~/WorkSpace/HomeAutomation/templates$
```

Now we can go ahead and edit the `main.html` file that we created in our home automation project and then save it as `Robot.html` file, as shown in following screenshot:

```
debian@beaglebone:~/WorkSpace/HomeAutomation/templates$ sudo nano main.html
```

Once you have opened the `main.html` file, using the nano text editor, edit the content to make it look like the following screen shot:

You can see that we have added the image source element from our previous topic into this HTML file and added four buttons. Once you have saved the file, you can go ahead and make the changes in the Python file that we need to run in order to create a server using Python.

First let us go back to the home automation directory:

```
debian@beaglebone:~/WorkSpace/HomeAutomation/templates$ cd ..
debian@beaglebone:~/WorkSpace/HomeAutomation$
```

Now let's open the `GPIOControlWebApp.py` file that we created in the home automation project:

```
debian@beaglebone:~/WorkSpace/HomeAutomation$ sudo nano GPIOControlWebApp.py
```

Edit the file as shown in the following screenshot and save it as `Robot.py`:

```
GNU nano 2.2.6                    File: GPIOControlWebApp.py                    Modified

import time
from itertools import cycle
from flask import Flask, render_template

import Adafruit_BBIO.GPIO as GPIO
GPIO.setup("P8_18", GPIO.OUT)
GPIO.setup("P8_16", GPIO.OUT)
GPIO.setup("P8_14", GPIO.OUT)
GPIO.setup("P8_12", GPIO.OUT)

app = Flask(__name__)

@app.route("/")
@app.route("/<state>")
def update_lamp(state=None):
    if state == 'F':
        print "Robot Moving Forward"
        GPIO.output("P8_18", GPIO.HIGH)
        GPIO.output("P8_16", GPIO.LOW)
        GPIO.output("P8_14", GPIO.HIGH)
        GPIO.output("P8_12", GPIO.LOW)
        time.sleep(.2)
    if state == 'R':
        print "Robot Turning Right"
        GPIO.output("P8_18", GPIO.HIGH)
        GPIO.output("P8_16", GPIO.LOW)
        GPIO.output("P8_14", GPIO.LOW)
        GPIO.output("P8_12", GPIO.LOW)
        time.sleep(.2)
    if state == 'L':
        print "Robot Turning Left"
        GPIO.output("P8_18", GPIO.LOW)
        GPIO.output("P8_16", GPIO.LOW)
        GPIO.output("P8_14", GPIO.HIGH)
        GPIO.output("P8_12", GPIO.LOW)
        time.sleep(.2)
    if state == 'S':
        print "Robot Stopped"
        GPIO.output("P8_18", GPIO.LOW)
        GPIO.output("P8_16", GPIO.LOW)
        GPIO.output("P8_14", GPIO.LOW)
        GPIO.output("P8_12", GPIO.LOW)
        time.sleep(.2)
    template_data = {
        'title' : state,
    }
    return render_template('Robot.html', **template_data)

if __name__ == "__main__":
    app.run(debug=True, host='0.0.0.0')

File Name to Write: Robot.py
^G Get Help        M-D DOS Format        M-A Append        M-B Backup File
^C Cancel          M-M Mac Format        M-P Prepend
```

Now you can run the Python code by using the following command:

- `sudo python Robot.py`

```
debian@beaglebone:~/WorkSpace/HomeAutomation$ sudo python Robot.py
 * Running on http://0.0.0.0:5000/ (Press CTRL+C to quit)
 * Restarting with stat
 * Debugger is active!
 * Debugger pin code: 142-692-876
```

Just running this code is not enough. We also need to run the streaming software to give our project the live video feed. So, login to the BeagleBone Black using another PuTTY session, and run the streaming software as shown in the following screenshot:

When the streaming software and the Python code are running simulatneously, you can go ahead and check the server file by pointing your BeagleBone Black's IP address at port 5000, from any browser, via a PC or mobile phone connected to the same local network same as to which the the BeagleBone board is connected. You will see the output shown in the picture on the next page, from where you can see the live feed and control the robot:

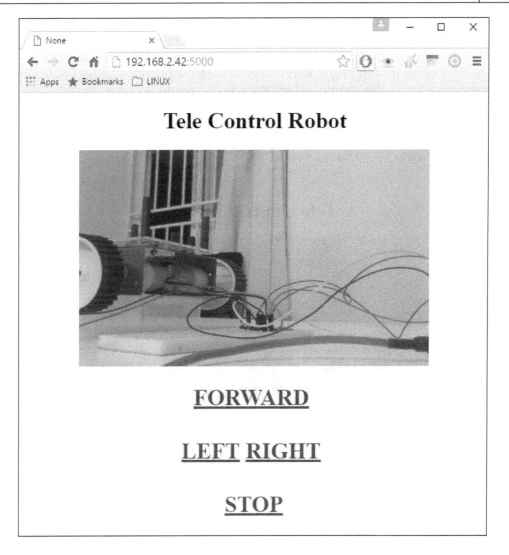

So, in the preceding screenshot you can see the robot's wheels. The setup is the same as that shown in the picture at the beginning of this topic, where the camera was pointing at the wheels of the robot. This will show you how the wheel movement works when you click on each button on the web page. We will discuss this next where you can see the wheel movement on the images themselves, as the wheel that is running will look blurred.

When you click for the forward button. Both motors run as discussed out previous chapter regarding the differential drive system. That is the motors will drive the robot in forward direction, you can see the difference in the following screenshot where the motors are running when compared with the previous image shown in the previous page of this chapter where the wheels are idle and not running.

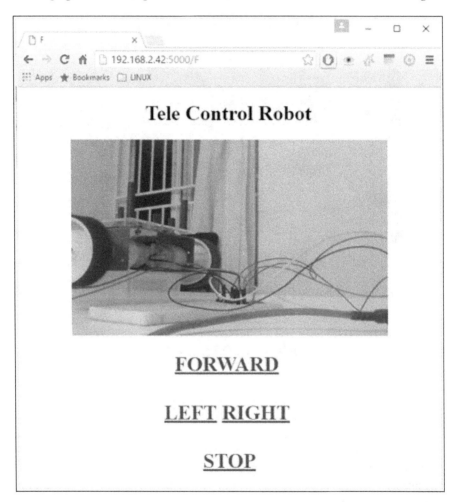

You can also see the log of the movement in the Python output when you press the button as shown in the following screenshot:

```
Robot Moving Forward
192.168.2.5 - - [09/Jul/2016 15:09:48] "GET /F HTTP/1.1" 200 -
192.168.2.5 - - [09/Jul/2016 15:09:49] "GET /favicon.ico HTTP/1.1" 200 -
```

Similarly, for turning left, the right motor needs to be running and the left one stopped, as shown in the following screenshot:

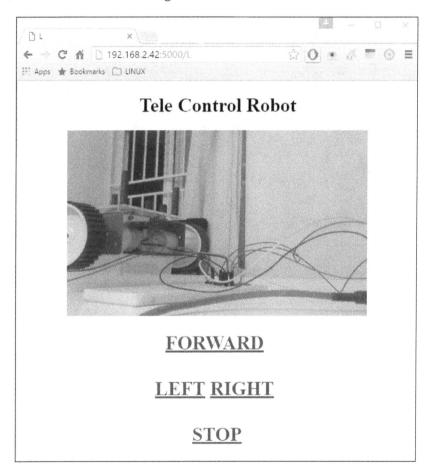

And when you press the **RIGHT** button then the **LEFT** motor is running, and the **RIGHT** one is stopped, as shown in the following screenshot:

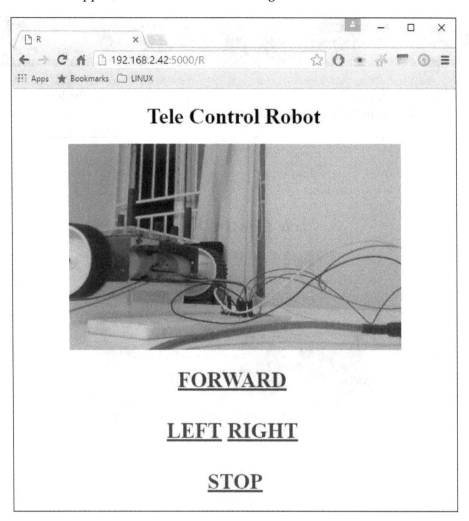

Similarly when you click on stop, both motors will be stopped. If you mount all these electronics on top of the robot as desired, you can make it drive around as a telecontrolled robot with a live feed carrying the BeagleBone Black with the camera. In this chapter I gave you all the resources you need to understand this idea. Now, you can go ahead and mount the electronics on the robot base. To find out how people make a simple prototyping shield with electronics soldered onto it on top of the hardware development boards. Just type in Google, `prototyping capes for BeagleBone` or `hats for raspberry pi and shields for Arduino`. Even though these are made for different hardware development boards like BeagleBone and Raspberry Pi, the same electronics can be mounted on a BeagleBone board with slight modifications which will help you get rid of the messy wiring. Also, try using the sub-process Python module to execute the shell command and start streaming software at the beginning of the Python code to start running the server. By using this sub-process you need not run two instances of PuTTY, you can finish your work with just one.

Summary

With that we are at the end of this chapter, where we have learnt some basics about DC motors and their operation, as well finding out what an L293D motor driver IC is, and how we can use it to control a connected DC motor connected. Next, we saw how to live stream video on the local server with BeagleBone Black using mjpg-streamer package. Finally we worked on a project where we interfaced the L293D motor driver IC with the BeagleBone Black, and a live streaming image source, to HTML templates and controlled a robot using the input buttons on the webpage that we created using the Python and Flask web server framework.

Index

H

home automation system
building, with BeagleBone 133
materials required 134
power switches 148-153
prerequisites 134
relays 148-153
structure 134, 135
transistors 148-153

I

image capture, from camera
Python and OpenCV used 177-183
Internet controlled power switch
about 154
AC bulb, controlling from Internet 154-157
port forwarding, setting up 157-164

L

L293D motor driver IC 217-219
LED
about 48
blinking, with Python script 63, 64
toggling, with push button 76-84
libraries
adding, to Python 55-58
Linux command-line interfaces
reference 33
Linux shell
working 33-36
live video streaming
on BeagleBone board 220-230
LM35 sensor
used, for temperature sensing 88-97
working 87, 88
ls command 33

M

medical robotics
about 207
reference links 207
microSD card
BeagleBone board, booting 20-24
preparing 14-20

mkdir command 34
mobile robots
reference links 208, 209
motion-based home security alert system
creating 194-198
prerequisites 186
motion detection
passive infrared (PIR) sensors,
using 189-192
Motor Controller IC 203

O

OpenCV
about 171
installing, on Debian on BeagleBone
board 171-177
setting up, on BeagleBone board 171
operating systems
installing 13-20
references, for Mac users 20

P

passive infrared (PIR) sensors
about 186
used, for motion detection 189-192
working 187, 188
physical computing systems
about 68
basic elements 69-75
LED, toggling with push button 76-84
usage 75
physical computing systems,
connecting to internet
advanced level project 123
e-mail alert fire alarm project 114-122
Internet access, giving to
BeagleBone board 100, 101
prerequisites 100
sensor data, uploading to
web cloud 123-130
Wi-Fi capability, adding to BeagleBone
board 101-114
pwd command 34
Python
libraries, adding 55-58

used, for accessing general-purpose input/output (GPIO) 58-62
Python-Flask
  about 137
  on BeagleBone Black 137-148
python interactive shell interface
  reference 37
Python Package Index (PyPI) 137
Python script
  used, for blinking LED 63, 64

R

Random Access Memory (RAM) 75
Read Only Memory (ROM) 75
real-time physical computing system
  building 85
  materials needed 86
  prerequisites 86
rm command 36
robot, building with BeagleBone Black
  materials needed 215
  prerequisites 215
robotics 200, 201
robotic systems
  elements 202-204
  operation 202-204
  structure 202, 203

S

Secure Shell (SSH)
  about 25
  BeagleBone board, logging over Ethernet 25-32
sensor data
  uploading, to web cloud 123-130
switches
  about 48
  creating 48-50
  momentary switch 50, 51
  toggle switch 52, 53

T

TCP/IP Network 136
telecontrolled robot, with live video streaming
  building 231-241
temperature sensor
  about 86
  LM35 sensor 87

U

Ultra Sonic Sensor 203
USB camera
  adding, to BeagleBone board 168-170
USB camera, interfacing with BeagleBone
  materials needed 168
  prerequisites 167

W

web servers 135-137
Win32 Disk Imager
  reference 16
World Wide Web (WWW) 136